**For Ella Krikler and the children who helped make this book:
Mia Aylott, Abel Rubinstein, Shannon Noone, Joshua Shaffer,
and Alice Softly**

Copyright © 2001 Zero to Ten Limited
Photographs copyright © 2001 Sally Smallwood
Text copyright © 2001 Sally Smallwood

Publisher: Anna McQuinn
Art Director: Tim Foster
Senior Editor: Simona Sideri
Publishing Assistant: Vikram Parashar

First published in Great Britain in 2001 by Zero To Ten Limited
327 High Street, Slough, Berks SL1 1TX

A CIP catalogue record for this book is available from the British Library.

ISBN 1-84089 196-3

Printed in Hong Kong

CAN YOU SEE IT?
TRIANGLE!

SALLY SMALLWOOD

TRIANGLES ARE

They have three sides
and three pointed corners.
Sometimes they point up,
sometimes down.
Turn the pages and see
how many you can find!

Here are lots to get you started.

Look
carefully...
triangles can
be hard to spot!

I've got triangles for my breakfast. Have you?

Fold a square of paper in half...

and you make a triangle!

Triangles play tunes.
One, two, three!
Do, re, mi!

My triangle
is a house
and a roof
and a slide!

I can make triangles with my arms!

Triangles are hard to find, but they are brilliant. Can you find them? Can you make some of your own?

MARC
CHAGALL

WERNER HAFTMANN

TRANSLATED BY
HEINRICH BAUMANN AND ALEXIS BROWN

THAMES AND HUDSON

Frontispiece: THE CELLIST. 1959. Ink wash and gouache, 23⅝ × 19⅝". *Private collection*

First published in Great Britain in 1985 by
Thames and Hudson Ltd, London

Reprinted in 1998

This is a concise edition of Werner Haftman's
Chagall, originally published in 1973

British Library Cataloguing-in-Publication Data

A catalogue record for this book is available from the British
Library

ISBN 0-500-08022-4

Printed in Singapore

CONTENTS

Marc Chagall

We think of Marc Chagall as the painter-poet of the twentieth century. He shares this distinction only with Paul Klee.

For a painter to transform both the visible world and human emotions into visual poetry might well earn him a title of honor, yet it was on this point that criticism of Chagall began. Aimed at the poetic side of his art, it consisted of accusations of infatuation with literary, symbolic, folkloristic, and religious ideas, and was voiced especially by ideologists of Cubist and Constructivist persuasion.

Such criticism, however, failed to take account of the point in history which had been reached, and hindered further development. By the end of the last century a new attitude to the visible world had become prevalent in all intellectual fields, and certainly needed a new language for its visual manifestation. The basic ideas had already been formulated by Cézanne and Seurat, Gauguin and Van Gogh, and thus for a time painters could concentrate their efforts on the formal and grammatical aspects. Certain tasks had been done: painting had been transformed, mainly through an emphasis on the independent aesthetic values of color and form, and a new organization of the picture had been developed by the replacement of the Renaissance perspective system with an aperspective and multidimensional system more in keeping with contemporary experience of the world.

Chagall came to Paris in 1910 at the age of twenty-three, and entered the arena of European painting with his pictures of 1911–12, which were his first great works. By this time Matisse and the Fauves, on the shoulders of Gauguin and Seurat, had already perfected the use of pure color for an expressive and balanced composition. And the Cubists, following Cézanne, had found a crystalline, aperspective pictorial architecture which revealed the harmony of forms underlying visible objects.

The next task in developing the new pictorial language was to fill out the newly found syntax with fresh imagery and previously inexpressible emotions, from the sphere of the unseen and the irrational. The landscape, the nude, and the still life, with which both the Fauves and the Cubists had developed the new syntax, were no longer adequate as motifs, and a powerful influx of new ideas was necessary. The French intellect had supplied the design; now was the time for elaboration.

Marc Chagall supplied just that. From his Byelorussian and Eastern Jewish origins, he brought into play entirely new vistas of irrational perception from dreams, visions, and legends. Such fantasy, which somehow lay beyond the reach of the French intellect, altered and enhanced the expressive power of color and the new formal organization of the picture.

The painters, especially Delaunay and his circle, were interested above all in Chagall's chromatism. His colors, lit up by the strange legendary radiance of Russian folklore, seemed to sing. The effect was quite different from that of the French use of color, which was based on theories of the objective and the rational. What interested the poets and thinkers, however, about Chagall was the unexpected widening of the intellectual horizon, in which images of dreams, memory, and fantasy became just as important as visible reality, and where even natural objects acquired legendary and mythical associations. "Supernatural!" murmured Apollinaire when he visited Chagall in his studio in 1913, seeking a name for the store of images from the unconscious and from dreamlike memory which filled the paintings. André Breton, the spokesman of Surrealism, came much closer to the mark when he later wrote, "In 1911, and through Chagall alone, metaphor made its triumphal entry into modern painting."

Pictorial metaphor meant nothing other than enclosing the imagery of experience, dream, or memory in a sequence of colored forms. One thing depended on the other. For its illustration, the poetic metaphor needed an analogous pictorial setting, built up by color and the formal construction of the picture. The pictorial setting, in turn, needed the poetic power of the metaphor for the extension of its range of inner meaning. This "poetry," then, for which a historically unaware and insensitive criticism has persistently reproached Chagall, was precisely the element which enabled him, at a particular moment in history, 1911–12, to suggest a new, poetic fullness for Cubism and thus save it from drifting into academic conventionalism.

But—and here I paraphrase a sentence from the other painter-poet, Paul Klee—a poetic idea becomes valid as a picture only when the painter finds the perfect means of uniting imagery and construction. This, then, was Chagall's problem. Because he found the solution, the poet Chagall could become a true picture maker and a European painter who could at last combine the form-conscious rationality of Western European art with the mysticism of the Eastern European soul. The intimate union of the pictorial and the poetic constitutes Chagall's originality. It is the nucleus of his pictures. Through this union his art became of signal importance for French Orphism and German Expressionism, as well as for the development of Surrealism.

Chagall himself wishes to be regarded as a painter; the constant references to him as a teller of fables and legends—as a poet, in short—make him indignant. Yet he has only himself to blame. This reputation is in complete accord with the whole style of his personality. When, at the beginning of 1912, he took up residence in La Ruche, the "beehive" of artistic bohemians in Paris, he quickly gained the nickname "*le poète*." And if one is confronted today by this small, vivacious, always slightly hallucinating man, with his blue eyes and curly tufts of hair and his incredibly mobile face constantly changing from serenity to sadness, from artful drollery to lightning intelligence, it is impossible to disregard the poetic charm of his personality, which so strangely oscillates between humble earnestness and unexpected spurts of clowning.

Some of it is disguise—and this too is part of his persona—serving as a refuge and a defense, to guard the vulnerable nucleus of his artistry. A glance into the studio is granted to only a few. Chagall is busy there from dawn to dusk, but few know what he is doing. There he keeps himself to himself, an alchemist engaged in what he likes to call the "chemistry" of his painting, a man of the Cabala constantly immersed in a flood of highly enigmatic imagery. In the middle of a conversation a pensive shadow sometimes falls on his face, and the thread of an anecdote becomes tangled. His imaginative

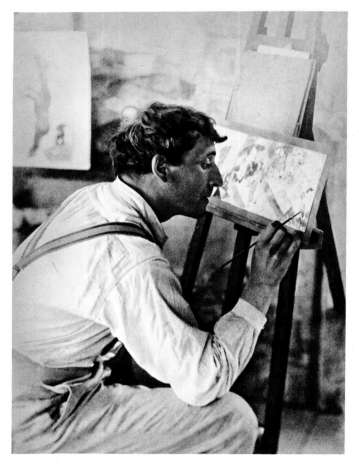

1　Marc Chagall, 1920–21

world has overtaken him again, and a sudden idea sends him into the studio.

Chagall always carries his picture world with him. He needs to have his paintings around him. Even on a short flight, as from his quiet house in Saint-Paul in Provence to Paris, he always takes his last works with him. When he returned to Paris from Russia and Germany in 1923, having lost all his early paintings, his first task was to repeat some of his old masterpieces in order to be surrounded once more by a horizon of his pictures. In 1941, escaping from Marseilles to New York and being in a very difficult situation, he snatched up every painting he could lay hands on. Like a snail he carries his house on his back; it makes him feel at home wherever he goes and is the sanctuary from which he can put out feelers for further reconnaissance of his world.

This method of reconnaissance is truly poetic. Chagall is totally filled with visions, with metaphors in response to the world, with inner images. For him, painting is the illustration of the inner world of images. Unlike Cézanne, he does not approach visible reality by means of an uninterrupted dialogue between the observing eye and the natural object to discover and depict the harmonious underlying forms of the object. He goes about it the other way: he approaches the as yet undefined picture from within; slowly, as the pictorial elements fall into place, he lets the painting materialize. Some paintings, such as *The Falling Angel* (colorplate 27), took decades to reach completion. Even when Chagall confronts nature directly, he likes to let observation drift into metaphoric allusion. All the small, tender marginalia—the lovers, fabulous beings, and musicians—that he loves to write around the edge or into the background of his flower pieces, landscapes, and portraits are hints at a further possible metaphoric meaning. They do not add anything in particular to the picture seen purely as a painting; instead, they are like annotations suggesting what poetic associations might still be made. The tenderness with which Chagall has painted the colors of a bunch of flowers, for instance, may unexpectedly evoke the image of a loving couple as a symbolic allusion to this tenderness.

In his personal life Chagall was on closer terms with poets than with painters. It is true that during the decisive years of 1911–12 he was friendly with Delaunay, knew Léger, and at Riciotto Canudo's (who was the editor of the avant-garde periodical *Montjoie!*) met the entire set of painters grouped around Delaunay, Le Fauconnier, and the brothers Villon. Later he came to know Picasso, Braque, and Matisse, and always kept in touch with them, but he remained outside all the painters' conventions and had an insurmountable fear of their theories. His best friend during the years in La Ruche was the poet Blaise Cendrars, who looked on with amazement as his painter friend managed to transmute the symbols of his fantasy into visual poetry by the orchestration of colored shapes. Cendrars penetrated so deeply into Chagall's fantasy world that he even invented titles for a number of his pictures. In the spring of 1913 Chagall was visited in his studio by Apollinaire, whom Herwarth Walden, the spokesman for the Expressionist Sturm group in Berlin, had commissioned to write a preface for a proposed exhibition of Chagall's work. The preface never materialized, but as a consequence of this visit Apollinaire went into the nearest café and wrote on the back of a menu a poem dedicated to Chagall.

Not only was Chagall acknowledged by his poet friends, but his art had far-reaching impulses for them. Cendrars' "Prose du Trans-Sibérien" and Apollinaire's poem "A travers l'Europe," both decisive incunabula of a new surrealist poetry,

2   Marc Chagall in Vence, 1965

avowedly owe their astonishing associative verbal imagery to the influence of the painter Chagall.

The most remarkable example of his affinity to poetry has been given us by Chagall himself. As a lad in the narrow circle of his Jewish family clan in a suburb of Vitebsk—in whose vocabulary the word "artist" simply did not exist—he had dreamed of becoming first a singer, then a dancer, then a poet, and finally a painter, and he set about writing his autobiography when he was only thirty years old! This undertaking, quite astonishing for a young painter, is nevertheless not too difficult to explain in the light of his artistic development. During his first years in Paris, homesick for his native Vitebsk, Chagall had relived in memory his whole childhood. Out of this background his pictures emerged as assemblages of individual remembered moments in his life, each memory in the metaphorical disguise of its own legendary overtone. Later, when Chagall went back to Russia and was again confronted with the reality of life there, he tried to preserve for himself the legendary nucleus of his original experience and to record it as poetic reality, in poetic language. His purpose was to weave the individual strands of memory, which had taken hold of him with hallucinatory power in the loneliness of his Paris studio, into the web of a complete poetic picture. His autobiography, *My Life*, is therefore far less a biographical report than a psychographical record which fills in the artist's background and establishes it as a poetic reality.

This is the background, poetic and humanistic, against which Chagall's paintings are outlined. If, time and again, Chagall was able to discover in reality the core of legend—the rag-and-bone man with his sack becoming the symbol of the wandering Jew (fig. 4), the begging itinerant preacher the symbol of the man of God (colorplate 13), the urban landscape of Vitebsk across the Dvina a vision truly out of this world (colorplate 14)—this was intimately connected with his hal-

lucinatory talent stemming from his carefully preserved and cherished sense of poetic reality.

What this was like can be seen from Chagall's autobiography, which was supplemented by his wife Bella's books of memoirs, *Burning Lights* and *First Encounter*, which she began writing

3   Marc Chagall painting the window of the cathedral in Zurich, 1969

about 1937. She pictures him as a sensitive, somewhat neurotic youth, whose clear-sighted gaze was able to penetrate the veil overlying a warm and familiar everyday life and see strange and wondrous aspects of the reality that surrounded him. He was introverted, dreamy, touchy, and affectionate, with a secret narcissism which made him tend to be a little eccentric in appearance and behavior. Full of fantasy, he experienced the excitements of childhood with such intensity that he remained aware of them throughout his life.

Born on July 7, 1887, he grew up in modest circumstances in the Jewish suburb of Vitebsk. His father was a hardworking assistant at a fishmonger's, a serious man and a devout Jew, who remained in Chagall's memory as a weary figure in a prayer shawl reciting the ceremonial prayers. His mother—short, lively, and strong-willed, a prototype of the Jewish mamma—kept the big family of seven sisters and two brothers together. She ran a small haberdasher's shop and made the decisions in all family matters, including little Marc's schooling and his artistic training, which at least she did nothing to hinder. It was an open house which hummed with domestic and neighborly activity. Innumerable uncles and aunts came and went, but the beggars, ragmen, and preachers who wandered through the Jewish communities could also expect a glass of tea. It was this often quite enigmatic world which animated Chagall's childhood imagination.

The house was down by the river Dvina, among other simple wooden dwellings with small vegetable gardens, courtyards, and backyards where fowl strutted, and goats, pigs, and a good-natured white cow wandered—in short, the whole menagerie which was to file through the painter's pictures in all sorts of fabulous disguises. He had a close relationship with the animals, talked to them, was amused by their quaintness, and looked upon them as companions and personalities, together with certain objects, such as the lamp or the samovar, which had for him a strangely personal character.

Relationships with his male comrades were rather shy and distant, though things went somewhat better with the girls. But not until he met Bella, a very poetic girl from a bourgeois Jewish background who entered his life at an early stage, did he find not only his life's companion but also the protection, affection, and shelter out of which he could look at the world in his own fashion, without fear.

Beyond the river lay the town, crowned by a monastery, cathedral, churches, and synagogues. The town remained the vista of home, which Chagall was to rebuild again and again right up to the works of old age, whenever remembrance struck a chord. This was how he had looked on Vitebsk as a child, when, hidden in the loft, he had peered through the dormer windows at the town. These glances out of the window, from the shelter of the inside—the inner world—into the alluring, glittering, and distant outer world, were his way of looking at life.

Observed from a distance and from hiding, the world took on an enraptured, magical, and legendary quality for Chagall. The street one was watching would turn into a stage, upon which unfolded the dramas and comedies of the Jewish suburban community. Its people all had something hallucinatory, caricatural, excessive about them, which emerged particularly when there were special occasions to be observed—birth, marriage, death. Then the collective feeling of the community manifested itself in laughter, dancing, shouting, and crying, which created patterns of gesticulating movement, so

that all was transformed into a play with many characters. But first would come the fiddler, followed by other musicians, and then, when the festivity was at its height, the town acrobats would appear. At this point, artistic fancy came into play and hung fairy lights on commonplace reality and its familiar characters, who seemed to emerge from an unreal, otherworldly sphere. These were the scenes and dramatis personae which have occupied Chagall's fantasy and filled up a good deal of his work (figs. 13–15).

Beyond the town stretched the open country, with rough tracks leading to the huddled cottages. Sometimes these roads ended in an open space with a cattle market, which swarmed with gesticulating, shouting, or loitering people—that whole bone-idle but highly poetic tribe of Russian peasantry which Gogol has so unsurpassably described. With his uncle Neuch, a cattle dealer, Chagall rode across the fields in a little rustic cart drawn by a pony, pulling up to collect a docile cow or a quaint little calf, and in the market place he marveled at the archaic figures of the peasants.

In the summer his mother sent him to his grandfather in a nearby village. The grandfather was a butcher by trade, a proper Russian who, as Chagall recounts, spent half his life lying on the stove, a quarter of it in the synagogue, and the rest slaughtering and preparing the animals. But he was also a true Jew, butcher to the Jewish community, who performed the ritual of slaughter in its religious, sacrificial form. The young Marc suffered with the animals when the knife plunged into their necks, but he also understood the meaning of the sacrifice. The picture of the sacrificed animal became strangely connected with a remote picture of a crucified creature as a symbol of suffering. "And you, little cow," he murmurs, "naked and crucified, you are dreaming in heaven. The glittering knife has raised you to the skies." In the moving painting *Flayed Ox*, 1947 (colorplate 28), this experience still lingers. The animals, the people, the wooden houses, the farm implements were all only variations on a great theme: its name was Russia, and it sank into his soul. To be a Russian painter—this he took upon himself as a conscious destiny, and looked

4 OVER VITEBSK. 1914. Oil on cardboard, mounted on canvas, 28¾×36⅜″. *Private collection, Toronto*

upon it during his country's darkest hours as his title of honor.

But he was also a Jew. One cannot compare suburban Vitebsk with the general notion of a ghetto, but there was no lack of regulation, discrimination, and anti-Semitic pronouncements in czarist Russia. When it had been decided that Chagall should attend the municipal school, it took all his mother's cunning and a few bribes to get around the ruling forbidding Jewish children to go to state schools. When he went to St. Petersburg to study painting, he had to pretend to be a servant in a lawyer's house in order to avoid the residence restriction on Jews. The outer world was hostile. Resistance also came from within the community, however, from the orthodox old men who looked with disapproval on their nephew's learning Russian at all. The grandparents of both Marc and Bella constantly grumbled about the newfangled thirst for knowledge. The traditional teacher was the rabbi. People read Hebrew and, to be sure, the Bible; but they spoke Yiddish and used Hebrew mainly to talk to rabbis, preachers, and wandering men of God about the meaning of God's word. Life's daily round was governed by prayer. The synagogue was the stronghold, and the prayer shawl and *tefillin* (the prayer bindings) were the insignia of communion with the holy. The virtues of the believer were withdrawal from life, submission to the incomprehensible will of God, and an extraordinary capacity for suffering. Thus in the memories of both Marc and Bella the father is an earnest figure, standing turned to the wall in his prayer shawl, rocking himself in the rhythm of prayer.

This intensely religious atmosphere permeated every aspect of life. Within the festal circle of the Jewish year—described as it was celebrated in Vitebsk by Bella in her book, *Burning Lights*—the history of the Jewish nation and the characters of the Old Testament took on a living reality. In the glow of the candles, the singsong of prayers, and the ritual preparation of the festal meal, only a breath would be needed, it seemed to

5   IN FRONT OF THE NATIVE HOUSE. 1908. Pen on paper, 6½ × 5½″. *Collection the artist*

6   THE BALL. 1907. Pencil on paper, 11¼ × 8½″. *Collection the artist*

the children, to bring to immediate life all the characters from the biblical legend. The miraculous waited at every corner; it was just under the surface, and there was nothing to prevent a messenger of God from crossing the threshold in the form of a beggar.

Eastern Jewish religious doctrine was deeply influenced by the Hasidic movement, as Martin Buber has informed us. The Hasidic tradition abounded in vivid parables in which the Zaddikim (Righteous Ones) wrapped their teaching around the omnipresent being of the invisible God. They presented a wondrous picture of God's love pouring into the basin of the world, which shattered into myriads of fragments in each of which remained a scintilla of God's love. Hence the simplest thing held miraculous possibilities, the world took on a translucent quality, and reality and legend intertwined. In the synagogue, where the young Marc was allowed to assist the cantor, and in the emotional exaltation of the devout Jews which overflowed into everyday life, the outer world took on a hallucinatory dimension. Its mystic light colored Chagall's vision and feelings in his youth, and was never to be forgotten.

Chagall does not care for too much emphasis to be laid on this religious aspect, yet it must not be left out of consideration, because it concerns his specific outlook on life and the specific store of images from which his paintings came into being. The matter must also be seen in a wider context: it is with and through Chagall that Judaism, which for thousands of years had eschewed all pictorial art, found its own individual artistic expression in pictures. Out of the special circumstances of modern painting, which generally was turning from outer to inner inspiration, he helped to cause the buried springs of

7 LITTLE PARLOR. 1908. Oil on paper, mounted on canvas, 8⅞× 11⅜″. *Private collection*

imagery in the Jewish soul to flow at last, and Jewish perception of the world, which had been confined to words, to be released in visual expression. This is an achievement of secular rank, and is there for all to see in the stained-glass windows of the Hadassah synagogue near Jerusalem.

The treasure of pictures and feelings which had deeply impressed him during his youth was something Chagall carried with him always. He took with him, as Bella so beautifully describes, "instead of an inheritance, the breath of his parents'

8 THE HOUSE IN THE PARK. 1908. Oil on canvas, 24×20⅞″. *Private collection*

house like a piece of his father's shroud." And Chagall himself confesses, "If my art had no place in my family's life, their lives and their achievements greatly influenced my art." This poetic golden background had to be made visible; there the biography of Chagall the painter begins.

Chagall had quite a good education. He learned Hebrew and biblical history from a rabbi; the Russian-language school added the rest. Though not a particularly good scholar, he was full of enthusiastic creative impulses. When he received singing lessons from the cantor, he wanted to become a singer. When Uncle Neuch scraped out a tune for him on the fiddle, it was clear he was on his way to the conservatory. Whenever something artistic was offered, he went into it with full enthusiasm. In the end, painting won the day.

Chagall had been drawing from childhood, and in that respect was at the top of the class. When a schoolfellow admiringly told him he was a real "artist," this word, unknown in the vocabulary of his family, struck him like a lightning flash. In Vitebsk there was a school of painting run by an artist called Pen, and here he took his first lessons. But these did not take him very far, and he worked mostly by himself. Some drawings of this period still exist, and are quite outside any academic compass. They show groups of figures—for instance, in a wedding dance (fig. 6), and peasants in conversation—rendered in a broad comprehensive style, with caricatural detail, clumsy but bold drawing, and a strangely naive conception.

In the spring of 1907 Chagall was able to enroll in a semi-public school of art in St. Petersburg, which soon brought him a small scholarship. Although he found his academic studies far from satisfying, he became acquainted with a number of Jewish intellectuals who helped him on his way and broadened his mental horizon. But not until he was able to attend the art school of the famous Léon Bakst, where he remained from the autumn of 1908 to the spring of 1910, apart from lengthy visits to Vitebsk, did he sense something of the breadth of art. In the cultural circles of contemporary czarist Russia, Bakst was seen as representing the avant-garde. In the face of historicism and realism he pleaded for an expressive painting style of decorative composition, in which melody of line and harmony of color counted more than descriptive quality, and which lay roughly between the Jugendstil of the Vienna Secession and the Symbolism of the French. Bakst was well acquainted with Parisian painting and liked to talk about it. In his company Chagall heard for the first time the names of the great innovators: Manet, Monet, Gauguin, Cézanne, Van Gogh, and Matisse. But all this was little more than rumors—"of new traditions, of Aix, of the painter with the severed ear, of cubes, of squares, of Paris"—as Chagall recalls.

That they were looked on as revolutionaries gave these artists a special significance. Just at the time of Chagall's years of apprenticeship, an urge to overthrow traditional artistic conceptions was swelling within the young Russian art, and this animated Chagall's search for a new personal expression. With the political uprisings of 1905 a new revolutionary climate had evolved which had a strong influence on the restless intellect of the new generation and gave rise to certain uniform characteristics, summed up by the term "Leftist art." Expressionism, Fauvism, Futurism, Cubism—these were the names by which one identified oneself.

The tie between the young revolutionary artists and the

9 YOUNG GIRL ON A SOFA (MARIASKA). 1907. Oil on canvas, 29½ × 36½". *Collection Ernesto Blohm, Caracas*

movements in the rest of Europe, including Paris, was very strong. By way of Kandinsky, who wrote articles for *Apollo*, and his Russian friends around the New Art Syndicate of Munich, the link with German Expressionism was established. Hardly had Italian Futurism been proclaimed in Milan than it was reflected in Moscow and St. Petersburg. In 1910, the first group of Russian Futurists, in which the poet Mayakovsky participated in a provocative role, had formed around the brothers Burliuk. Fauvism, principally associated with the name of Matisse, and Cubism, with that of Picasso, had already made their influence felt with amazing liberating power. The first exhibition of the Fauves was held in Moscow as early as 1907, and ever since then the name of Matisse had haunted the studios of the young painters. All the revolutionary changes in France, exemplified by such movements as Symbolism, Divisionism, Fauvism, and Cubism, were reflected almost immediately in the centers of Russian culture. During this close intercourse with western modernism, the new Russian art evolved.

The first groups were formed in 1907–8, and were still connected with Jugendstil and Symbolism. The group of artists calling themselves the Heaven-Blue Rose, which included Chagall's teacher Bakst, gave the first exhibition of this symbolist aesthetic in Moscow in 1908. Their aim was to remove from colors and forms their realistic function of objective description, and to handle them "as music does its tunes." In this analogy to music, referred to by painters time and again since Gauguin and Redon, was a growing consciousness of the independent expressive capacity of pure colored forms. At the same time, a deeply expressive style of painting, strongly primitive in character, was beginning aggressively to thrust Symbolism aside. This new style was brought before the public eye in an exhibition put on in Moscow in 1908 by a group of artists associated with the magazine *The Golden Fleece*. It stressed formal issues: the expressive line of the simplified contour, the expressive force of pure unbroken color, the ornamental arrangement of the surface. The influence of the French Fauvists was unmistakable, and was combined with

the expressiveness the painters had discovered in the bright colors and decorativeness of Russian folk art and in the naive drawing of Russian shop signs.

By this time the dams were broken. In the autumn of 1909 the vigorous new talents were on view at an exhibition in St. Petersburg organized by the Union of Youth. The names appearing there are now synonymous with the Russian artistic revolt: Larionov, Goncharova, Tatlin, Malevich, the brothers Burliuk. Their common style was an ecstatic Fauvism, rendered in bold unbroken colors and primitive, simplified outline. Almost simultaneously the influence of Futurism and early Cubism had an effect. In St. Petersburg the brothers Burliuk propagated a style derived from both movements, which they called Cubo-Futurism. In Moscow the group of painters known as the Jack of Diamonds put on another exhibition which was already, as a contemporary critic put it, "unified by the cult of the cube." These exhibitions triggered off the wildest disputes about modern painting. A leading critic of the period described the situation in 1911: "The gods change from day to day. Cézanne, Gauguin, Van Gogh, Matisse, Picasso, even Van Dongen and Le Fauconnier, are being plundered without sympathy, restraint or discrimination. It is a pandemonium where everything is turned topsy-turvy. Everyone tries to shout the loudest in order to appear the most modern."

The young Chagall from provincial Vitebsk could of course only watch these turbulent developments from the sidelines. Nevertheless, he may have found some confirmation of his drastically simplified drawing, the naive forcefulness of his imagery, and his ornamental arrangement of the surface in these diverse and to him quite unfamiliar ideas.

That his own creative thoughts were moving in a similar direction, however, can be seen from some of his works of that

10 RED NUDE SITTING UP. 1909. Oil on canvas, 36¼ × 28". *Private collection, London*

11 THE HOLY FAMILY. 1910. Oil on canvas, 29⅞×25″. *Collection the artist*

period. There is a small study in oils of 1908, *Little Parlor* (fig. 7), in which the flat expanses of color and the decorative arrangement of the outlined objects clearly indicate experiments in the manner of Matisse. Landscapes, on the other hand, echo a dark symbolistic element which recalls paintings of the group associated with Gauguin in Brittany (fig. 8). A solidly constructed nude (fig. 10), set four-square on the canvas, reveals his preoccupation with the pictorial problems of surface, form, and space.

Chagall's main work consisted of portraits and compositions with figures. In the portraits he sought the simplest form and set it broadly and serenely on the canvas, enlivening it with a rustic setting. In regard to influences, one can compare, for instance, the very personal portrait of his little sister, *Young Girl on a Sofa (Mariaska)*, 1907 (fig. 9), with the portraits by Paula Modersohn-Becker or with those by the lyrical naturalists of the Pont-Aven group around Gauguin. But the young Chagall saw the work of Gauguin only in poor reproductions without color, and had to bring it to life and significance through his own imagination. Gauguin's influence can also be seen in Chagall's figural compositions, which include rustic scenes with a few thickly outlined figures, their gestures wooden, who are shown huddled together. For his themes—*The Circumcision, The Holy Family* (fig. 11), *The Couple* (fig. 12)—the artist took scenes from his surroundings and gave them a kind of symbolic meaning. Slowly and awkwardly, the Chagall iconography begins to stir in them.

In addition to these pictures, some remarkable hallucinative paintings made their appearance in this period. One such phantasmal scene is *The Dead Man*, 1908 (fig. 13), where, in the dark village street, a body lies on the ground among funeral

candles, a lamenting woman hurries away, a street cleaner unconcernedly carries on with his job, and a man on the roof plays the fiddle. This quite unreal scene, of great simplicity, is the artist's visionary response to an experience he had had very early one morning, when at first light a woman ran down the village lane loudly lamenting the death of her husband. The coloring is dull and dark; only the soap-green sky gives the scene a spectral light. Closer to familiar reality is the painting *The Birth* of 1910 (fig. 15), showing the confined woman with the midwife under a red canopy, while whispering Jews are awaiting the event in the golden circle of lamplight. The black of night looks through the windows into the room, which is illumined by flickering, fantastic light. A gleam of Rembrandt falls upon the homely scene.

In these paintings, there is a search for the pictorial expression of the enigmatic and legendary aspects of reality. But despite the expressive simplification and the reduction to essentials the means are still naturalistic. Color is still restrained, still tightly bound to objective description.

Yet there remained Matisse, the saint of Aix, the painter with the severed ear, the alluring promise of Paris! In 1910 Bakst had left Russia to join Diaghilev in Paris, and that was a stimulus to Chagall. A patron in St. Petersburg was prepared to grant him a small allowance, and the urge to become a painter drove him to Paris, the "Mecca of painting."

Chagall arrived in Paris in the late summer of 1910. He was overcome by the liberal atmosphere of this city and by its light, the *"lumière libcrté,"* as he never tired of calling it. With the help of Russian friends he was able to stay in a compatriot's empty apartment in the Impasse du Maine, but by early 1912 he had moved into a studio in La Ruche (The Hive). This was a grotesque cluster of cheap, rather dilapidated studios grouped around a twelve-sided hall, in which the cosmopolitan bohemians of Paris found refuge. Here Chagall remained until his

12 THE COUPLE. 1909. Oil on canvas, 35⅜×39⅛″. *Private collection*

departure in the spring of 1914 for Berlin and Russia, and here started his major pictures.

In the beginning, the artist's yearning for his native Russia made it hard for him to settle down. Only in the Louvre did he find reassurance. Like Cézanne before him, he stood in wonder before the works of Veronese and saw how, by a silvery luster of color and the ornamental pattern of the surface, he had transformed the world into art. There were also Manet's dazzling canvases, strongly confined to the surface, Delacroix's tightly woven web of color, Courbet's robust definition of reality. Many things attracted Chagall: the severe regularity of Fouquet, which veiled a secret mysticism; Rembrandt's brilliant manipulation of chiaroscuro, in which the glow of light transported the scene into the realm of fantasy; the mysterious aura in which Chardin enveloped simple things.

Once the Louvre let him go, he trotted tirelessly through the galleries—Durand-Ruel, Bernheim, Vollard—and there he saw the masters whom till then he had known only from hearsay: Cézanne, Van Gogh, Gauguin, Matisse. The most exciting thing of course was coming face to face with the young French art. The very first day after his arrival, so Chagall tells us, he hurried to the Salon des Indépendants and made his way "to the very heart of the French painting of 1910." With unfailing eye he at once turned to the two principal movements, Fauvism and Cubism. The one showed the most uninhibited treatment of color, the other a crystalline, fragmented structure of the surface which created an aperspective, independent spatial construction in which the natural object fitted into a formal pattern. To be sure, he felt a degree of criticism—an uneasiness at the rationality of French art, its intellectual treatment of color, and its insistence on the analysis of visible forms. "I had the feeling," he recalls, "we are still only skimming over the surface of the matter, that we are afraid of plunging into chaos, of breaking up the familiar ground under our feet and turning it over." Nevertheless, there was no doubt that here in Paris a new conception of art had arisen.

Outside the galleries and museums Paris itself lay all around him. Daily he made his way on foot through the city, marveled at the light, lost himself in the teeming life of the streets, and filled his lungs with the atmosphere of freedom and equality —something taken for granted here, but which put him, a Jew from czarist Russia, into a state of euphoria. Here he was a free man and, moreover, an artist, a word which only here took on its full meaning. In this elated condition he took in Paris—with the amazed eyes of a stranger who was separated by the language barrier from the blunt reality of life. So it was as if he looked through a magic crystal—and he absorbed everything he saw.

When he began to work again, with the effects of Fauvism vivid in his mind, he too wished to experiment with bright, intense colors arranged in balanced surface patterns, and the influence of Matisse is recognizable. But a joyous ecstasy seized him that overrode orderly color arrangement and disciplined composition. Outbursts of pure color blazed up, the brushstroke became uneven, the ornamentation rolled across the surface. An irresistible desire for self-expression rebelled against the discipline he sought.

A good example of this process is evident in the painting of his studio (fig. 16), one of the more tranquil pictures of the year 1910. It was begun as a calm arrangement of areas of harmonious colors. A color harmony based on green was intended to build up the unity of the surface, with the light color values illuminating the spatial planes formed by the

13 THE DEAD MAN. 1908. Oil on canvas, 27⅛×34¼″. *Private collection*

14 LA KERMESSE. 1908. Oil on canvas, 26¾×37⅜″. *Private collection, Santa Barbara, Calif.*

15 THE BIRTH. 1910. Oil on canvas, 25⅝×35¼″. *Collection the artist*

16 THE STUDIO. 1910. Oil on canvas, 23⅝×28¾″. *Collection the artist*

distant color values. This pointed in the direction of Matisse. But in spite of Chagall's efforts to remain within this intellectual discipline, his hallucinatory temperament ran away with him during the process. In the lower right the construction begins to sway, the blue console table gives an unruly lurch, and then, like a grotesque apparition, the broad wicker chair pops up like a grimacing clown in the midst of the ensemble which began with such orderly intentions. The visionary element

17 THE MODEL. 1910. Oil on canvas, 23¼×19¼″. *Private collection, Paris*

shatters the ornamental harmony like an Expressionist eruption.

The conflict between discipline and ecstasy characterizes all the work of 1911. From this period there is a number of Fauvist studies of nature motifs, figures, and nudes. But gradually these fell into the background as an entirely different wellspring of imagery began to bubble inside Chagall. He had brought with him from Russia a few canvases painted with large figurative scenes of life in Vitebsk, and he revised these according to his new ideas of painting. This work revived old memories; fantastic scenes came to mind, the irrational undermined familiar surfaces, the view of the world was violently changed. This intrusion of the fantastic exploded in the great but absurd painting (if considered from a logical point of view), *Dedicated to My Fiancée* (fig. 18). It shows a confusion of limbs and broken utensils heaped upon the surface, with a man sitting in their midst, leaning his bull's head on his hand and calmly allowing a woman to sling her thighs around his shoulders and spit lovingly into his mouth. A large round shape like the end of a trombone blows into the bull-man's ear. In the lower left is a female leg, suggesting startled flight, and to its right, a fragmented oil lamp. The contents of the picture are not open to logical scrutiny; they are the metaphor of a condition, which the reader may choose to interpret as symbolic of a sexual obsession. In its basic concept the picture was painted one night while the artist was in a hallucinatory condition, using a flood of superimposed associative images without the interference of consciousness. This invasion of the irrational opened the door for a profusion of imagery, lying like humus in the soil of memory. As to form, it is highly interesting to note that in this painting of rapture the "surface as place of appearance" is already evident, and Cubism with its patchwork elements and fragmented planes has made its first entrance.

This most important period in Chagall's work entered its decisive phase at about the time he moved into his new studio in La Ruche in 1912. The background out of which his pictures materialized now changed radically. The outer world sank back, and in the glow of memory emerged a transfigured Vitebsk. The *Self-Portrait with Seven Fingers* of 1912–13 (fig. 19) shows his psychic situation. The painter sits before his easel, his back to a window through which Paris is seen, and with his large, fan-shaped hand caresses his votive painting to his homeland, *To Russia, Asses, and Others* (colorplate 5). Above this, like a heavenly vision, floats Vitebsk. On the wall he has written, in Hebrew—the solemn confessional script of his youth—the words "Paris" to the left and "Russia" to the right, but he has his back to Paris! Remembrance has overtaken him again and is sublimated in pictures which reproduce the faraway, remembered land of childhood in highly poetic metaphors.

We often say that memory makes everything beautiful. But the memory picture does more. It gives to the reality of our experience a legendary quality, and it filters out of the confusing multiplicity of real experiences the essential elements—that is, those which concern the essence of our being.

Moreover, removed from the restrictions of space and time which subjugate our ordinary way of life, memory is multi-dimensional: spatially separate experiences flow together into a total picture; separate time levels become transparent and overlap. Because of its synchronal quality, by which separate events appear simultaneous, memory makes experienced reality appear comprehensive, like a many-faceted crystal. It creates an *imago*; being a composite picture laden with mythical and metaphorical elements, this *imago* obviously is not something that can be *reproduced*, like a realistic motif—it can only be *evoked*. It first materializes in the act of painting, coming forth from the mind as a chain of associative images, including the revelation of the invisible, to form the total picture. This procedure required a completely new approach to picture making, which until then had been built on the interpretation and reproduction of the visible.

In this situation, Cubism came to Chagall's aid. With Cézanne as their starting point, the Cubists had laid the groundwork for the structure of the new evocative picture. For them, the picture was no longer a window opening on to nature; instead, it was an independent field of vision, in which the unity of the surface was of first importance. With the fragmented arrangement of overlapping planes—the *plans superposés*—the surface was transformed into an independent picture space devoid of perspectival illusionism. Thus the picture was created out of spatial impulses and movements rippling like waves or advancing in delicate gradation across the surface. The content of light in the planes themselves, with their color and chiaroscuro, provided the illumination; an independent, inner picture light took the place of a representation of natural light. Objective description was reduced to simple emblems of things, which fitted into the general design as formal elements and could be modified accordingly. The transparency of the planes allowed several views of the object, such as full face and profile, to be combined and more or less superimposed, thus giving an account of the entire structure, which was fundamentally lacking in perspectival representation. This approach brought motion into play; rhythmic movements on the picture surface were created by the sequential arrangement and development of single formal statements, and this independent rhythmic quality took the place of copied processes of movement. Thus all the categories out of which the picture was built and which until then had all tended toward the reproduction and interpretation of visible reality—surface, space, light, composition, and rhythm—were radically converted in the direction of pictorial independence. The new picture's function was no longer to reproduce and interpret, but simply to evoke. It did not render visible reality, but made visible the inner response of the human being to reality.

Chagall, through his study of Matisse, had already learned much about the importance of independent surface, color, and ornament. Then he encountered the Cubist construction of the picture, with its crystalline architecture lit up by an inner radiance. With sudden understanding, it seems, he recognized the possibility of making visible his own imaginative and remembered world, which was also lit up from within.

The fact that Analytical Cubism, because of its preoccupation with the architecture of the picture, had foregone vivid colors in favor of a subdued color scheme was of lesser importance to Chagall; meanwhile, in Cubism itself, an undeclared secession had occurred which called for a resurgence of radiant color contrasts in the crystalline structure. It was known as Orphic Cubism, and its leading exponents were Delaunay and Léger. Chagall very soon became friendly with Delaunay, and the association with this experienced colorist must surely have influenced him to orient himself more exactly in color theory. In turn, Chagall's sensitivity to the lyrical expressiveness of color had its effect on Delaunay. Léger, whose painting *Les Noces* of 1911 could have been one of the pictures which gave Chagall his sudden enlightenment about the possible scope of Cubist picture construction, was introduced to Chagall by Canudo. The art of the Orphists was something Chagall could respond to, for in its radiantly colored lattice the natural motifs moved into a further dimension, as if they were apparitions perceived in the distance of legend. Helped by such means, Chagall found

the road open for him to give visual expression to the ideas, lit by the glow of memory, that filled his mind. The only stumbling block for him was the Orphists' calculated rationalism in dealing with colored forms and a certain realism which still persisted in the analysis of natural motifs, whether landscape, still life, or figure, leaving out of account the whole inner picture world of fantasy and memory. For him, the Cubist picture space, structured of superimposed transparent planes, became the magically translucent colored stage on which his images of memory and dreams could make their appearance.

He made a discovery about the *plans superposés* which was decisive for him. These transparent planes, which the Cubists used for the definition of surface area, were interpreted by him in a personal way as psychic levels: they became forms which corresponded to the transparent planes of dreamy memory, or layers between which the strata of memory could be freely inserted. The simultaneous views, which for the Cubists meant the synchronization of separate views of the object, became for Chagall superimposed recollected images and dreams. With these means he saw the possibility of making the complex

18 DEDICATED TO MY FIANCÉE. 1911. Oil on canvas, 77⅛×45". *Kunstmuseum, Bern*

picture of his ideas, composed of countless separate remembered images, totally visible. The separate memory images became interlaced with the structure of the surface planes. The eye followed the individual stations of memory and rediscovered, in the evocative setting of the picture, the unity and totality of the poetic image awakened in response to memory. The picture surface had become the stage where remembered reality made its appearance in metaphorical disguise; memory was metamorphosed into painting.

Chagall does not analyze objects, he analyzes his memories. He has said, "My pictures are painted collections of inner images which possess me." The individual inner images are shaken up as if in a magical kaleidoscope, and in the context of the picture they function like substantives, each evoking a long chain of memories. Thus a naively defined prospect of Russian houses and domed churches stands for the poetic background of Vitebsk; milkmaid, cow, or mower evokes the country life; a Jew with his sack, ritual tokens, and various scenes conjure up the Jewish legends; star symbols and abstract constellations in space bring cosmic associations. From "key words" such as these the poetic sentence is put together.

This process, though, has nothing whatever to do with literature. The images are made concrete only by the expressive arrangement of colored forms in the pictorial design. Indeed, they can develop only in association with the resonance of colors and the rhythm of forms, and can achieve truth and probability only when they make their appearance in the picture. Because of this Chagall feels himself free "to overturn the usual surfaces"; thus, some of the details may quite well turn upside down, if this is what the surface arrangement suggests. Seemingly disparate material can find surprising connections, and dimensions can be out of all proportion, since the individual fragments are only emblematic allusions. Through this *"dérèglement de tous les sens,"* as Rimbaud called it—through the derailment of logic and consciously directed perception—the road was opened to the throng of pictures submerged in unconscious memory.

The strangest inventions, whose pictorial imagery is nevertheless easily readable, now appeared in Chagall's paintings. For instance, in *To Russia, Asses, and Others* (colorplate 5), we find an enormous milch cow, suckling both calf and child and standing like a droll statue on the tiny roofs of a Russian village, while out of the cosmic radiance of the sky a maid leaps forth like a messenger from heaven; in her haste, her singing head becomes detached from her body and contemplates with awe the sublimity of the firmament above the Russian countryside. This extraordinary scene, in the magical revelation of the picture, is the metaphor for the emotion aroused by the memory of Holy Russia.

The poetic radiance of these paintings and their indivisible unity of content and formal structure can only be appreciated by contemplation of the pictures themselves. I should therefore like to refer my readers to colorplates 3–10, which show some of the major works in this cycle of paintings, and to the accompanying commentaries in which I have attempted to describe their formal construction and the significance of their contents. What can be learned from this is the discipline with which Chagall took possession of the already formed characteristics of the evocative picture of the Cubists and the extraordinary hallucinatory power through which he filled up the new pictorial structure with poetic metaphors. This, over and above the visualization of his personal existential experiences, is Chagall's historic achievement: that, immediately perceiving the evocative possibilities of the Cubist picture, he opened it

up to embrace the irrational world—the imagery of the unconscious, of dreams, and of memory.

Apart from the poets, he received only a hesitant response from his French associates. The painters were intrigued by his expressive color, which to them gave his paintings a somewhat phantasmagoric quality. The critics, rather taken aback, felt the undertaking to be too "literary." At the root of it all was the rationality of the French intellect, which resisted the invasion of irrational conceptions. In fact, Chagall's contempt of logical deduction and the emphasis he placed on the unconscious excitements of the soul are thoroughly Russian. He was moved by the age-old Russian mistrust of being guided only by conscious reasoning—Tolstoy had called it "the greatest moral evil," Dostoyevsky had felt it to be a "disease," and Gorky had spoken of "Russian distrust of the power of the intellect." This alogical and irrational approach to life, and the receptivity to the stirrings of the unconscious which went with it, meant that Chagall could radically transform the familiar mental images. Only after a slow process of learning, accelerated about 1920 by the effects of Dada and Surrealism, was French criticism prepared to recognize Chagall's achievement. When he returned from Russia to Paris in 1923, he was a famous painter.

The work Chagall was doing accorded with ideas current in German Expressionism, so it was not by chance that his first one-man show, in the early summer of 1914, was held in Berlin. In March of the previous year Apollinaire had introduced Chagall to Herwarth Walden, the spokesman of the Expressionist Sturm group, who reacted immediately. Already in the

19 SELF-PORTRAIT WITH SEVEN FINGERS. 1912–13. Oil on canvas, 50⅜×42⅛". *Stedelijk Museum, Amsterdam*

20 JEW IN BLACK AND WHITE. 1914. Oil on cardboard, mounted on canvas, 39⅜×31⅞″. *Private collection, Geneva*

21 JEW IN RED. 1914. Oil on cardboard, mounted on canvas, 39⅜×31½″. *Private collection, Geneva*

First German Autumn Salon in Berlin in September 1913, where the whole galaxy of the European avant-garde was assembled and in which Franz Marc played an influential part, Chagall was represented by three of his major works: *Dedicated to My Fiancée* (fig. 18), *To Russia, Asses, and Others* (colorplate 5), and *Golgotha* (colorplate 10). The November edition of *Der Sturm* published the two poems by Cendrars dedicated to Chagall. In June 1914 came Chagall's individual showing at the Sturm Gallery, and the painter went to Berlin for the opening. This exhibition established his fame.

Modernist Germany was prepared to receive him. Ideas very similar to Chagall's had been circulating in the Blaue Reiter group of 1911–12. Franz Marc, in his series of great animal pictures which began in 1911 and culminated in 1912–13 with the *Tower of Blue Horses* and *Animal Destinies*, was painting a new legend of the animal and its life in integral relationship to creation. Through a trancelike awareness of nature, he tried to arrive at a visionary penetration of the visible, so that the division between the self and the world was lifted, and the spiritual background to reality, which Marc called the "mystical inner construction," was revealed. Marc's elective affinities corresponded to Chagall's. In 1912 Marc wrote, "Cézanne and El Greco"—reproductions of both were pinned on the wall of Chagall's Paris studio—"are kindred spirits. The works of both these men stand today on the threshold of a new epoch of painting. Both felt the mystic inner construction behind the visible world, which is the great problem of today's generation."

There was also Paul Klee, whose art of free fantasy expressed in the wandering line could conjure up the picture store of the unconscious and of buried memory, which he called his "primordial field of psychic improvisation." Both Marc and Klee had become familiar with Orphic Cubism through Delaunay, whom they had visited in 1912 in his Paris studio. Both had immediately grasped the significance of the evocative picture, but—like Chagall—they sought to make use of the new means for the visualization of respondent images from within. The deep-seated romanticism within them found here the appropriate means of expression. It is not difficult to imagine with what interest these two questing spirits may have stood before Chagall's paintings in the Autumn Salon. Perhaps it was they who encouraged the Berlin collector Köhler, patron of the Blaue Reiter group, to acquire Chagall's *Golgotha*. It was in this intellectual context that Chagall acquired the rank of a European painter, who in his work expressed the intellectual tension between the visionary strength of Russia, the rationalism of France, and the romanticism of Germany. Germany found him a painter after her own heart, and thanked him by giving him his first fame.

The Berlin exhibition was also of particular significance in Chagall's personal life story. Once he had left Paris, he wanted to see his homeland and his fiancée Bella again. Having arrived in Vitebsk in the middle of June 1914, he was overtaken by the outbreak of war and was unable to return to Paris. At first he stayed at his parents' house, marrying Bella in the summer of 1915; then, to avoid active service, he moved to Petrograd, where he found a niche in the bureau for wartime economy. After the October Revolution of 1917 he returned to Vitebsk, where in the summer of 1918 A.V. Lunacharsky appointed him Commissar of Fine Arts for the district of Vitebsk. At the beginning of the following year he organized an academy of painting, and invited Lissitzky and Malevich, among others, to join him. He soon had a fierce dispute with Malevich, however, who wanted to establish his own ascetic constructivism, reduced to a few geometric forms, which he called Suprematism, as the ideological basis. Chagall gave up his appointment in May 1920 and moved to Moscow, where he became mainly concerned with the Kamerny State Jewish Theater; this formed the biographical framework of a new period of work. During the years in Russia from the summer of 1914 to the summer of 1922 his style changed remarkably.

At the beginning Chagall was completely captivated by the physical reality of his native environment, which in his memory had been transfigured into a legendary world. Now reality caught up with him once more. He portrayed everyone who came his way, painted landscapes and scenes from his surroundings, and in this way tried to document reality. But much as he tried to fit in with this solid reality, his visionary way of looking at things would not let him. Simple occasions—the entry of an old Jew into his parents' house, an odd happening in the street—could suddenly give rise to a visionary penetration of reality. I have tried to describe the process in the commentary on the *Jew in Green* of 1914 (colorplate 13). But there are other pictures of the same year for us to consider. In the *Jew in Black and White* (fig. 20), the portrait of the eternal Jew at prayer fits into the abstract sculptural arrangement of the surface like an icon in modern dress. In *Feast Day* (fig. 23), in a bare and formal setting, a grave Jew appears in front of the temple steps with the attributes of the Sukkot feast, but on his head stands a strange diminutive version of the same figure.

23 FEAST DAY. 1914. Oil on cardboard, 39⅜×31¾″. *Kunstsammlung Nordrhein-Westfalen, Düsseldorf*

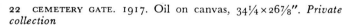

22 CEMETERY GATE. 1917. Oil on canvas, 34¼×26⅞″. *Private collection*

Over Vitebsk (fig. 4) gives a view of the street leading past the cathedral, while obliquely across the sky wanders the figure of a Jewish peddler with his sack, the ancient symbol of the outcast Jew's existence. These irrational eccentricities serve not only to establish the mood of the scene more emphatically through a poetic metaphor, but bring reality itself into a wondrous dimension. Yet there is also some pictorial reality in these scenes; the street of Vitebsk, lying deserted between the frozen cubiform houses and the church, is exactly defined, and in *Feast Day* the abbreviation of the synagogue entrance is a simple, archaic definition of the pictured object.

One could regard these characteristics as the expansion of the Cubist formula into reality, and yet there is something more—a remembrance of the impressive portrayal of reality by the early Florentines. On one of the pictures of this series, the *Jew in Red* (fig. 21), Chagall has inscribed the names of his masters. Unexpectedly, we find in the list the name of Giotto. The kind of ideas linking Chagall with the marvelous Tuscan artists of the early Renaissance can be gathered from his autobiography, written during the Russian years. Almost without exception, he uses the great early Florentine masters for a comparative description of his perceptions. When he wants a striking simile to indicate his Vitebsk, with its churches, houses, and synagogues, he calls them "simple and eternal, like the buildings in the frescoes of Giotto." In order to describe his father's face, he asks, "Have you ever seen one of those men in Florentine paintings...?" When he tells the story of a relative who paraded along the street wearing nothing but a shirt, this absurd scene appears to him: "... as if a painting by Masaccio or Piero della Francesca had come to life on the streets of Lyozno in broad daylight." Thus his outlook in those years was greatly influenced by the memory of the grandeur of form of the early Italians. It finds expression in the hard precision and archaic simplicity of the pictured objects, and in the magical serenity of form, which is what Chagall wished to point out when speaking of the "simple and eternal" quality of Giotto's paintings. This way of looking at things means that, in Chagall's work, familiar nature becomes its magical opposite, celebrating its own existence in solemnity and rapture. Chagall was now developing within himself a feeling for the "original solidity of things" (Carrà), similar to that which led, at about the same time in distant Ferrara, to the Italian *pittura metafisica*.

Certainly the structural basis of his paintings continued to be the evocative picture developed from his association with Cubism, and in 1917 the Cubist element seemed to become accentuated once more. In *Cemetery Gate* (fig. 22) the crystalline structure reappears in full force and binds the realistic elements into an abstract arrangement of luminous planes. But in other paintings—*The Blue House* (colorplate 14) or *The Promenade* (colorplate 15)—the Cubist medium is employed cautiously as a means of more closely approaching a vision of reality. A major work of 1917–18 is *Double Portrait with Wineglass* (fig. 24), which, for all its high-spirited metaphoric allusions, is a salute to classical painting and indicates a painterly attitude leading toward entirely new developments.

This transformation of the Cubist medium indicates a new preoccupation with formal problems. The disputes about Suprematism and Constructivism, which with the aid of Malevich and Tatlin were on the verge of becoming the "style of the Revolution," also left their marks on Chagall. When in 1920 he moved to Moscow, elementary abstract geometric forms and a flatness of the surface occurred again and again, which clearly indicates that his mind was affected by these matters. But all this overlapped with a new experience—that of the theater. Chagall came into contact with the Jewish Theater, painted scenery for a few plays, and, once at work, busied himself with decorating the auditorium with vast murals.

The theater! For Chagall it was the counterpart to his dreams, a pure realm of art in which eloquent movement, light, color, music, dance, and acrobatics all came into play. Here logic was of no account; fantasy paraded with full claim to reality, the imagined and the actual were interchangeable. The theater did not reproduce life, but presented it anew. In the largest of his murals, the *Introduction to the Jewish Theater*, Chagall has painted his own mental picture of the theater. Broad colorful trails of light travel across the enormous canvas (about 13×39 feet), and whirling shapes of prismatic color rotate over the surface. In this setting figures of dancers and musicians are in fantastic motion, while from the left the director leads on the theater painter himself. In the middle, around a colored circular shape, revolves a group of dancing Russian musicians. Then the scene shifts to a circus arena, in which acrobats are at work in a whirling medly. They stand on their heads, it is true, but as gravity and spatial perspective do not count, their upside-down position could be the normal one. The encounter with the theater gave Chagall the opportunity to paint vast figurative scenery, which gave full scope to the free play of his fantasy. His enlarged compositions of 1917 were in the manner of murals

and had involved experiments in abstract geometric forms, which later found confirmation in the wall decorations of the Jewish Theater. A summary of the achievements of these Russian years would certainly include, for one thing, the enhancement of the evocative picture with the material of reality, and for another—and this virtually through acquaintance with the theater—the triumph of the great figurative composition. From now on, all the many-figured compositions were to have a particular scenic character, as though the canvas were a stage.

By this time Chagall was growing tired of the constant discussions about art in Russia. He had never been keen on the so-called Revolutionary Art, and when in 1922, in reaction to what Lenin called the "intellectual confusion of Leftist trends," Socialist Realism became purely propagandist in its aims, it repelled him. He wanted to return to Paris, and in the spring of 1922, with the help of Lunacharsky, succeeded in getting permission to leave. After a short stay in Lithuania he journeyed to Berlin.

24 DOUBLE PORTRAIT WITH WINEGLASS. 1917–18. Oil on canvas, 91¾×53½". *Musée National d'Art Moderne, Paris*

25 FLOWERS IN MOURILLON. 1926. Oil on canvas, 38⅞×31½".
Private collection, England

26 IDA AT THE WINDOW. 1924. Oil on canvas, 41⅜×29½". *Stedelijk Museum, Amsterdam*

During his stay in Berlin, which lasted a year, he was particularly concerned with contacting Walden and searching for the pictures he had left behind in 1914. As a result there were unpleasant scenes, because Walden had already sold the major part of the paintings; the proceeds, which had been deposited with a lawyer, had been largely consumed by inflation. On the other hand, Walden had done a great deal for Chagall. The first of his *Sturm* Pictorial Reviews of 1919 was dedicated to Chagall, and in his pamphlet *New Painting* of the same year he stated categorically, "Art manifests itself primarily in the pictures of Kandinsky and Marc Chagall." Meanwhile, the paintings which he had sold had made Chagall famous. Young painters like Max Ernst and Kurt Schwitters had looked at them with deepest admiration.

The visit to Berlin would have remained a mere episode had not Walter Feilchenfeldt, the director of the Cassirer Gallery, offered to bring out Chagall's autobiography, *My Life*, concluded in 1921, which was to be illustrated with etchings. Owing to translation difficulties the book was not published then, but a folio of twenty etchings was produced. They show scenes and figures in Chagall's new naive-realistic style, and are executed in drypoint, the simplest engraving technique. This was the first time Chagall had come in contact with the reproductive graphic techniques; he became very enthusiastic about them and tried hard to exploit all the possibilities, including woodcuts and lithographs. His narrative flair had now found the right medium for its expression. Thus the work of Chagall as a graphic artist began in Berlin, but, curiously, it was a graphic assignment which led him back to Paris.

The editor Vollard, through the mediation of Cendrars, had invited Chagall to do some book illustrations, and Chagall requested that the book should be Gogol's *Dead Souls*. By September 1, 1923, Chagall was back in Paris and started to work immediately. In the short span of two years a series of 107 fine etchings was made (see figs. 64–68). In style they are akin to the Berlin drypoints, but the etching technique is more elaborate, and they are enriched by various refinements. The subtle tones give them a rich texture corresponding to the effects which Chagall then sought in his painting. As he worked on Gogol's pages, he found his own Russian themes once again. Moreover, he was longing to have the lost pictures from his first years in Paris around him again. Thus he made a series of repetitions, replicas, and reconstructions of the earlier paintings, so that he could reestablish his familiar pictures as his spiritual environment. During this process new themes evolved which had connections with the murals of the Moscow period. With all their fantasy, they show a greater objectivity in brushstroke and a loosely unfolding color.

But the really significant happening of the Paris years, which should not be obscured by the ever-recurring Russian *leitmotifs*, was Chagall's discovery of the real France. As was the case on his return to Vitebsk, he looked on his environment with new eyes. So far he had known only Paris; now he discovered the French countryside. During the years up to 1930 he never missed an opportunity of going into the country. His experience of the landscape of France, with its plenitude of light and the marvelous nuances of color radiating through a fine gray mist, changed his painting. He discarded the bright, poster-art colors, moderated the contrasts, smoothed the sharp-edged planes, and broke through the glassy foreground which lay like a magic windowpane in front of the Vitebsk landscape, so that the natural motif was made near and tangible. The color was laid on spontaneously and more plentifully. As

27 THE BEAR AND THE GARDENER. 1926–27. Gouache on paper, 19½×15¾″. *Collection Mrs. Lisa Arnhold, New York City*

28 THE FOX AND THE GOAT. 1926. Gouache on paper, 20×15¾″. *Private collection*

a result, a color web of delicate iridescent hues falls slowly over the planes, which had been bright and sharp-colored, like a sumptuous garment draped over the supporting skeleton of the picture. Intimacy with the French landscape prepared Chagall's senses to perceive this luminous web of color as something fundamental to the painting, structurally and emotionally, and the concept that color and design are really one thing. This perception matured toward the end of the 1930s and continued to influence all his later work. The paintings of Monet and Bonnard gave considerable support to this development.

In addition to painting landscapes, Chagall made his first independent flower pictures (fig. 25) in these years. They show a tranquil and loving absorption in the wonder of creative nature, and also little amorous marginalia—loving couples, animals, musicians—which adorn the painting, especially around the edges, like poetic interpolations. This is a theme which henceforth runs through Chagall's whole work.

Out of this harmony with nature was born the plan to illustrate the *Fables* of La Fontaine. Vollard was perfectly agreeable. Thus in 1926–27 Chagall painted more than a hundred gouaches, which spring from rather than illustrate the *Fables* and form a witty and delightful picture sequence of animal antics. Freshly and spontaneously painted in the full *élan* of first inspiration, they are uninhibited improvisations, showing more trust in the dancing brushwork and the allurement of color harmonies than in the logic of an already familiar tale. They were intended as pattern illustrations, to be made into color engravings by experienced technicians. When this plan misfired, in 1928–31 Chagall repeated them as black-and-white etchings. Out of this materialized his richest graphic

cycle, which, by involving every conceivable etching technique, reached that sumptuous painterly quality to which Chagall aspired (see figs. 69–72).

In addition to these fabulous tales of country life, the circus also received Chagall's attention. Once again it was the perceptive Vollard who steered him in that direction, with a commission for a folio of circus paintings. This is the most exuberant, impossible, grotesque circus one could ever imagine. Like goblins escaped from the wall of the Moscow theater, figures and objects whirl and tumble in the midst of extraordinary scenery. But unlike the flat multicolored Moscow decorations, these paintings have impasto, laid on as a thick, broad web of color. And around this group of improvisations on themes of fables and the circus there is a whole series of pictures on subjects and scenes dear to the artist, such as *Donkey with Eiffel Tower* (fig. 29).

These were good, happy, and busy years. Chagall was by then a celebrated painter, belonged to society, and fully enjoyed for the first time the festive life of glittering Paris in all its emancipation and elegance. This accord with the festive side of life is reflected in his painting. Already in 1924 there were pictures of a comparatively classical attitude and elegance, such as the *Double Portrait* with Bella. They culminated about 1930 in such consummately beautiful paintings as *Equestrienne* (colorplate 21) and *The Acrobat* (fig. 30).

The chromatic web now became quite tight, consisting of small particles which interact like pieces of mosaic to produce a glitter of color-light. Thus the garment of the acrobat (fig. 30) is made into a web of blue-red-green patterns interspersed with yellow—touching on the whole range of the color cycle—but all is so arranged and distributed that a luminous red-

29 DONKEY WITH EIFFEL TOWER. 1927. Gouache on paper, 25¼ × 19¼". *Collection Benedict Goldschmidt, Brussels*

painting of far-reaching significance. In the summer of 1934 he traveled to Spain, where he studied Velázquez, Goya, and El Greco. The year 1937 found him in Italy, where he stood contemplatively before the paintings of the Venetians. In these dialogues with El Greco, Goya, and Titian developed the idea of paintings on a larger scale, with a wider orchestration of color and greater depth of meaning.

A new source of material, which agreed perfectly with this conception, appeared at just the right time; this was the picture world of the Bible. Once again it was Vollard—who gave the impression of a sleepy water buffalo yet had the finest perception of the innermost emotions of his artist friends—who almost nonchalantly, as was his fashion, brought up this subject. He suggested Chagall should illustrate the Bible with a series of large etchings. Chagall responded immediately to the idea and, in quest of a starting point, traveled to Palestine for two months in the spring of 1931. The solemn beauty of the Holy Land affected him very deeply, as did the inspiration of its splendid light. He immediately started on the project, which was to continue as an important part of his future work. By the time World War II broke out, which roughly coincided with the death of Vollard, sixty-six plates were ready, and thirty-nine more were in the making (figs. 59–63).

As with the *Fables*, in many cases Chagall first prepared

30 THE ACROBAT. 1930. Oil on canvas, 25⅝ × 20½". *Musée National d'Art Moderne, Paris*

violet is produced as an immaterial color phenomenon. This color effect stretches over to the background of the market place, where it subsides through blue and green into darkness, and lightens up again, on reaching the sky, to a whitish illuminated blue. Thus, even out of the richest combination of colors is produced a floating, glittering, almost monochromatic color-light which, because the interaction of the contrasts ultimately tends toward gray, puts a transparent blue-gray haze over the picture. In this floating light the figure of the girl acrobat is delineated by a steady contour, filling out the decorative arrangement of the surface as she poses in the classical attitude. Calm and beautiful, she faces the onlooker; to emphasize the metaphorical meaning, a youthful messenger from heaven kisses the lovely *artiste*. The nature of the color sequence and the calm setting suggest words that previously would never have arisen: beauty, charm, and elegance.

Meanwhile, since about 1931, the scene was beginning to change. Times had become more difficult. The smoldering economic and political crisis which beset the European countries also brought various worries for Chagall. The persecution of the Jews began and took on systematic forms in Nazi Germany. While on a short trip to Poland in the spring of 1935 he experienced nasty scenes revealing the old deep-rooted hatred of the Jews which he had forgotten about during the years in Paris; these happenings made him feel strongly aware of his Jewishness once more. This change in atmosphere aroused in him the desire for a deeper, more serious kind of

31 THE REVOLUTION. 1937. Oil on canvas, later divided by the artist

the scenes in gouache; the painterly quality of the etchings, with their dramatic light and shade, reflects this procedure.

The selection of the Bible illustrations does not follow any prearranged iconographical scheme. There are many familiar scenes, showing the relationships among the biblical figures themselves or with holy messengers; there are moving portrayals of the enlightened or lamenting men of God; and there are also some quite unusual illustrations, such as Jeremiah in the cistern or a prophet killed by a lion. It is as if an apocryphal storyteller were describing an apocryphal text. The legendary figures, massively outlined and often shown half-length, dominate the scenes, which are dramatically presented—in settings from cloudy darkness to sudden bursts of light, producing a solemn and tragic mood. This cycle of illustrations, continuing year after year, marked the beginning of the development of the religious side of Chagall's art, which had its crowning glory in the pictures of the Biblical Message of the 1960s on.

Of course, during these years the loving couples, the flower pieces, and the circus scenes were not neglected, and Chagall's style of painting was often tender, bright, and serene. But the tendency was toward larger design and a surface built up of broader areas of color. A comparison of *Equestrienne* of 1931 (colorplate 21) with *Midsummer Night's Dream* of 1939 (colorplate 23) very clearly illustrates this development.

Chagall's main efforts went into a series of very large figurative compositions over which he toiled for years, although in the end he cut some of them into pieces. Behind it all was the ever-present desire, kindled by the memory of El Greco and Titian, to paint many-figured scenic pictures; this impelled him time and again, despite all setbacks, to attempt large-scale designs. He began in 1933 with the 78-inch-long canvas entitled *Dedicated to My Wife*, which shows a reclining nude surrounded by a variety of figures and scenes but remained unfinished, and continued with *Circus People*, 118 inches in length, which he later divided into two. This development reached a climax with the enormous enterprise of *The Revolu-*

tion of 1937 (fig. 31). This gigantic canvas, painted in the bloodiest years of the Spanish Civil War, renders the events of that time as the artist understood them; in his picture-book style he endeavored to organize great masses of figures and to describe them in a remarkably naive realism. Later, he cut this immense canvas into three parts.

Of these many-figured compositions there remain the tragic ex-voto of *White Crucifixion* (colorplate 22) and paintings such as *The Martyr* of 1940 (fig. 34). In the latter, against a background of burning houses a Jew clad in the tatters of his prayer shawl stands tied to the stake, a lamenting Jewish girl at his feet, while an old Jew intones psalms. What had happened is plain to see. The force of political events had dragged the painter along with it, making him invent a vision of terror compiled of scattered individual realistic details which, like a naive believer, he presents as a votive offering to the powers of fate. At this point Titian had certainly moved into the background.

In the spring of 1940 Chagall moved to Gordes in Provence; this was the first stage of his enforced departure from France. In the winter, through the representative of the American Aid Committee, Varian Fry, he received the invitation of the Museum of Modern Art in New York City to go to the United States. At first Chagall declined to leave France, but some warning experiences made the seriousness of the situation clear to him. In April of 1941 he journeyed with Bella and all his pictures to Marseilles and then proceeded to Lisbon, where he embarked for the United States. On June 23, one day after the German troops marched into Russia, Chagall and Bella arrived in New York. In his luggage were *White Crucifixion* and *Midsummer Night's Dream*—the visionary composition as votive offering and the mythical-fantastic picture like a sumptuous tapestry of color.

Cut off from his former life, Chagall became completely absorbed in his painting. In the beginning he lived in New York

32 THE RED COCK. 1940. Oil on canvas, 28⅜×35⅞″. *Private collection, Ohio*

33 THE FIRE. 1939. Gouache on paper, 19×25⅞″. *Collection J. Shapiro, Chicago*

City, but soon began to long for the countryside and moved to Connecticut, with its far-reaching wooded hills and solitary landscape.

He continued his work where he had left off—with the picture cycle of the *White Crucifixion* and *The Martyr*. He felt it was of high symbolic significance that his arrival in America coincided with the entry of the German troops into Russia. Russia was enveloped in war and the home of his childhood was falling to ashes, and this was a constant source of grief to him. Many pictures of this time show burning villages, crucified Jews in deserted streets, and apocalyptic scenes in which the innocent creatures of nature and myth—horses, cocks, and hybrid beings—participate as pathetic mourners lamenting the common suffering of the world to heaven, whose fiery darkness covers the misery of the terrestrial zone.

These pictures, without particular aggressiveness, present the Calvary stations of man, a victim under the scourge of hate. Here, in many variations, the figure of the crucified dominates. Like a shrine or a processional banner, it appears in the midst of scenes of devastation as a symbol of the healing presence of a being subjecting himself to God's decree and taking upon himself the suffering of the world. In order to emphasize the link between the Jewish concept of God and the Christian Messiah, Chagall always includes candelabra, a Torah roll, or Jewish attributes of prayer in association with the Christ figure (figs. 35, 39).

But even the pictures with circus scenes, with figurative and fantastic inventions, which carry on Chagall's old iconography, show the same intense seriousness and the nocturnal, terrifying apocalyptic mood. The scene is often set in a heavenly region, in which fantastic visions of animals represent mythic nature. In *The Three Candles* (fig. 37) the figures of a bridal pair, Chagall's old iconographical emblem for loving togetherness, float up into the heavens, fearfully clutching each other and looking back startled upon the earthly zone, which is fatefully illuminated by three candles. In *The Wedding* of 1944 (fig. 36), they stand close together under the fragile shelter of the canopy, but above, oppressively occupying more than half the picture surface, there is a concert by gigantic

angels, whose music does not seem to create a spirit of festive gaiety. There is the somber power of El Greco in these visions. *The Red Cock* of 1940 (fig. 32) makes portentous use of the animal metaphor: the enormous red cock, led on by a startled man flying through the air, struts across the moonlit sky to warn the animal musicians and their scared human companion hiding under a tree of coming disaster. These pictures, like *White Crucifixion*, show how reality can be enhanced by myth.

As for the development of Chagall's broad and rich orchestration of color, such as we find in *Midsummer Night's Dream*, this received a stimulus from an unexpected source. In the spring of 1942 the Russian choreographer Léonide Massine asked Chagall to design the scenery and costumes for his ballet *Aleko* in Mexico City, where Chagall went to work in August. The project also involved painting four vast backdrops, for which Chagall chose landscapes with immense skies (colorplate 24). These wide prospects gave him at last, within the unreal and free dimension of the stage, the opportunity to paint in broad sweeps of color. As in Turner's landscapes, the colors sail and whirl along like cloud formations, and out of these movements of color alone there arises a cosmic vista, surrounding the happenings on stage with a poetic atmosphere. Figures, animals, and constellations materialize from the color movements as symbolic interpretations of the chromatic harmony. They are not directly connected with the action on stage, but seek rather to express a pictorial response to Tchaikovsky's music.

The liberating influence of working with color on a grand scale enabled Chagall to make even more powerful use of color in his easel pictures. This was the moment when he left behind him the allegory of the reality pictures, which in the series on war and crucifixion had occasionally clouded his painting, and entrusted himself entirely to his personal mythology, which was introduced and developed by the evocative power of color.

Already in 1939 we find such pictures as *Time Is a River Without Banks* (fig. 38), which elaborate a pictorial metaphor by means of an apparently random collection of object-symbols. In this case a winged monster-fish, playing a violin, is flying over a river landscape in the company of a wall clock, its pendulum swinging. The strange-sounding poetic title given the painting at a later date fits the metaphor perfectly. *The Red Cock* of 1940 continued this use of metaphor. It led in 1943 to *The Juggler* (colorplate 25), the first *tableau manifeste* of the American years and the starting point of a new cycle of hermetic picture parables; its significance is discussed in the commentary. The crystalline kaleidoscopic structure which Chagall had begun to use about 1911–12 was now at last dissolving and giving way to an expansion of color embracing the whole picture, so that the skin of color encompasses the structural skeleton and covers it.

While this decisive pictorial development was taking place, Chagall received a harsh blow. On September 2, 1944, Bella, who had been the guardian of his domestic and inner life from the beginning, died. For months he could not find the strength to work. When at last in the spring of 1945 he resumed painting, he returned to the neglected large composition *Circus People* of 1933, in which Bella appears as sympathetic muse, cut it up, and made two pictures out of it. These again celebrate the figure of Bella—as a bride entering another world (colorplate 26) and as a grief-stricken entranced

mourner, in whose lap an angel puts the crystal ball of memory.

In the course of this work Chagall came across *The Falling Angel*, which he had begun in 1923 and had put aside for many years. At last, as a consequence of knowledge gained in painting *The Juggler*, he completed this picture in 1947. *The Falling Angel* (colorplate 27) is the crowning point of the American years. Its parable relates to the fateful experiences of the age. In this painting the artist has expressed the needs and longings, the frustration and hope, the fear and faith of the times, so that through its poignant imagery the viewer can understand the human essence of those years. Just as Picasso's *Guernica* stands as prophetic warning at the beginning of that terrible decade, Chagall's *Falling Angel* stands at the end—a visual parable of essential life experiences as filtered through memory, which was Chagall's source of imagery from the start.

By this time Chagall's pictures had become truly embedded in color. Their expressive power radiantly supports legendary parable and gives to objective description a poetic meaning. Again it may have been the theater which had this liberating effect on Chagall's handling of color. In the summer of 1945 he did the scenery and costumes for Stravinsky's ballet *The Firebird*, organized by the New York Theater Ballet. In these

34 THE MARTYR. 1940. Oil on canvas, 64¾×44⅞″. *Private collection*

35 DESCENT FROM THE CROSS. 1940. Gouache on paper, 19⅛× 13″. *Collection Mrs. James McLane, Los Angeles*

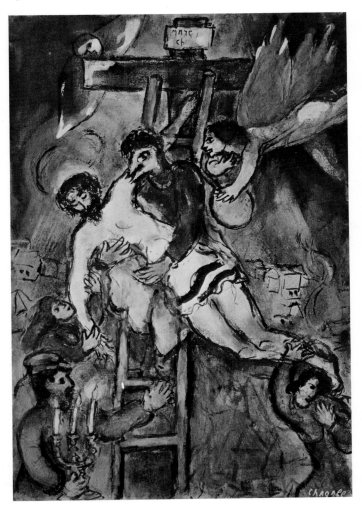

36 WEDDING. 1944. Oil on canvas, 35½×29¼″. *Private collection, Bern*

stage designs the melody of color is carried into almost abstract strains (fig. 40). Never again did Chagall reach such paroxysms of color.

But by this time he felt he must return to Paris.

Shortly before Bella's death, both had listened breathlessly to the news on the radio of the liberation of Paris and had joyfully contemplated the fastest possible way of returning there. In May 1946 Chagall was in Paris for a few months, and in the autumn of the following year the Musée National d'Art Moderne mounted a comprehensive exhibition of his work. In August 1948 Chagall returned to France to make his permanent home there. For a while he lived at Orgeval near Paris, but passed the winter months at Saint-Jean-Cap-Ferrat near Nice. In 1950 he settled in Vence, and by the springtime was in his own house—a tree-surrounded villa called La Colline on the edge of the township. Finally, in 1967, he moved into a newly built house in the tranquillity of a wooded valley in the neighborhood of Saint-Paul. In these surroundings, which have a faintly Grecian air about them, ripened the work of his later years.

Chagall had now become settled. It is true that he constantly traveled to Paris, revisited Israel in 1951, spent a few weeks in Greece in 1952 and 1954, and made occasional journeys to Italy. Later on, important commissions necessitated journeys to Israel and the United States, but nevertheless his major artistic work was carried on in the peaceful studio in the Midi.

Chagall soon made contact with the publisher Tériade, editor of *Verve* and heir to Vollard, who began to publish in quick succession series of illustrations left behind by Vollard. In 1948 *Dead Souls* was published, in 1952 the *Fables*, and in 1957 the Bible illustrations, the etchings for which Chagall had completed between 1952 and 1956 (see figs. 59–72). It was also Tériade who in 1952 invited Chagall to illustrate for him the antique pastoral romance *Daphnis and Chloe*, which induced Chagall to pay his first visit to Greece.

At the same time an important event happened in the personal life of the painter—his marriage to Valentine (Vava) Brodsky in 1952. Together they traveled to Greece, to the island of Poros, where, in the wonderful light of the Greek summer which completely captivated Chagall, and in the poetic light of the ancient love story of Daphnis and Chloe, his new life cycle began in that companionship which he needed for his preservation.

The character of this work and the development of Chagall's easel pictures are discussed in the commentaries to the color-plates. The easel picture alone, however, was no longer the center of his work. The painter was ever more strongly moved by the idea of assembling his works to create an artistic whole, and he frequently thought about art in cyclical terms. When Chagall began work in his new studio at Vence in the spring of 1950, he commenced with the biblical theme. *King David* was created as the starting point of a cycle, to be gradually followed by episodes in the life of Moses of the same monumental composition. Chagall's desire to paint these great canvases had been kindled by making the biblical etchings.

But there was more to it. During his strolls Chagall had discovered on a hill the Calvary chapel, which was surrounded by beautiful trees and was to the west of the township, with a crossroad fringed by little chapels leading up to it. This enchanted spot gave him the idea of restoring the half-ruined building as a place of worship by decorating it with pictures of a Biblical Message. This was the first time that Chagall was seized by the idea of filling one place entirely with his own pictures, expressed in his personal iconography. The whole series of biblical paintings was made with this idea in mind, and so, for instance, were the four striking pictures inspired by the *Song of Solomon I* (fig. 41) which he began painting in 1957 for the sacristy of the Calvary chapel and which were meant to be dedicated in remembrance of Bella. But this noble plan of decorating the chapel was never executed. It was only later that the city of Nice took up the idea, and in 1971–72 erected a new building in the right wing of which the pictures of the Biblical Message find their home as a bequest of Marc and Vava Chagall.

Meanwhile in 1952, during work on the biblical picture cycle, which was pursued steadily over more than two decades, Chagall conceived the idea of a new series. Just as previously he had celebrated his native Vitebsk, the painter now wished to pay his personal tribute to Paris. Work on the Parisian series went on for two years, during which time the city landmarks were celebrated in poetic *vedute* like scenes from a

37 THE THREE CANDLES. 1939. Oil on canvas, 50¼×38″. *Collection The Reader's Digest, Pleasantville, New York*

38 TIME IS A RIVER WITHOUT BANKS. 1930–39. Oil on canvas, 39⅜×31⅞″. *Museum of Modern Art, New York City*

summer night's dream, complete with lovers and fabulous creatures. In June 1954 the Galerie Maeght showed the twenty-nine pictures under the title "Homage to Paris."

During these first years in Vence the painter began to branch out into various new techniques. At first this seemed to be a mere amusement, and only later could it be seen as a logical development of his work. It all began in 1950 with ceramics. Pottery workshops were plentiful in the neighborhood of Vence. It was the mysterious chemistry of earth and fire, out of which the color is sintered, as it were, that attracted him, and what further delighted his painter's eye was the inner radiance of color obtainable only by this technique. The color shining through the glaze, obtained only in the process of firing and not directly affected by the painting hand, had that luminous, immaterial quality which Chagall was seeking in his easel pictures. The series begins with simple plates, plaques, and vases which, in accord with the themes of his painting, are decorated with biblical scenes, fabulous beings, lovers, and circus motifs, followed by Parisian themes to match the Paris cycle (figs. 43, 44). Very soon Chagall also made larger panels consisting of several ceramic plaques put together. Although the greater part of his ceramic work was done between 1950 and 1955, he has continued to occupy himself with this technique, which underlines its importance as a part of his experiments in color.

His intense preoccupation with color lithography may be seen in the same light. This had already begun during the last years in New York with the series of illustrations for the *Arabian Nights*. By 1951 it had become a major interest and from then on closely accompanied the painted work. In the process of building up the lithograph out of separate color

planes and bringing them together in the overprint, experiences could be gained which would further the development of his painting.

In his pottery, Chagall had first worked on readymade pieces, but soon felt he wanted to model his vases and vessels himself. These tended to be made in swelling, baroque shapes whose ambiguous character suggested anthropomorphic or animalistic forms, which then by means of color were marked out in certain directions and became nudes, figures, or fabulous beasts. This kind of procedure was familiar to him also in his easel painting (figs. 45–47).

Out of this intermediate stage between pottery and sculpture grew the first terra-cotta sculptures, and from these in turn grew the first sculptures in stone, which began in 1952. There are already more than thirty of them, mainly of marble, although Chagall has also used sandstone and tuff. They are of quite small proportions and generally designed as reliefs; even when they are stelae or short cylindrical shapes, meant to be seen in the round, they retain the character of reliefs. Their subjects are mainly half-figures—King David, Moses, Christ—or double-headed combined forms. Their style and subject matter recall late-Romanesque architectural designs, and indeed these carvings were intended as part of an architectonic context (figs. 48–51).

A favorable opportunity of putting new techniques to wider use came through a commission. Father Couturier, who had secured the services of a number of celebrated modern artists—including Bonnard, Braque, Léger, Matisse, and Rouault—for the decoration of the church of Notre Dame on the Plateau d'Assy, invited Chagall to decorate the baptistery, which stood apart and was connected to the main building only by a

39 THE CRUCIFIED. 1944. Gouache on paper, 24½×18⅝″. *Collection Mr. and Mrs. Victor Babin, Cleveland*

40 THE FIREBIRD. Sketch for stage curtain for Stravinsky's ballet. Gouache on paper, 14⅞×24⅜". *Collection the artist*

Roman arch. Chagall completed this assignment in 1957. He decorated the main wall with a ceramic mural ten feet high and eight feet wide; it was composed of ninety plaques and showed Moses dividing the waters of the Red Sea. The color, based on a harmony of blue, is cool and light and is applied to the wall as a tiled surface. Two carved marble panels, 43¼″ wide, are fitted into the side walls. They are in inverse relief, and their rich ornamentation modulates the cool light of the wall. The finely chased designs show in one a bird that has just escaped from the snare of fowlers, and in the other a hart at the water's edge, as illustrations to Psalm 124, verse 7, and Psalm 42, verse 1. A new technique, that of glass staining, now came into play for the first time. Chagall decorated each of the two side windows, approximately 40″ high, with a flying angel. Both windows are almost monochromatic, the design is delicately applied, and only a few yellow accents enliven the matt whitish light. Modest as this application of the glass-staining technique may be, it is the beginning of a road which leads Chagall's conception of color, irradiated and immaterialized by the changing effects of light, to the very summit of achievement.

In the small baptistery Chagall for the first time had had the opportunity of filling a whole room with his art. It is of no little significance that for this work he employed nothing but the so-called artisan techniques. It is as though a long-dormant talent in craftsmanship had awakened in him, and from then on he seized every opportunity of applying his art in public places.

There was no shortage of commissions. Closest to the easel pictures were the interior decorations he was invited to do for public buildings. They began with the circus and theater panels for the foyer of the Frankfurt Theater and culminated

in the panels for the ceiling of the Paris Opéra in 1964. For this colossal task Chagall summoned the whole pantheon of his muses and their fabulous attendants and filled the enormous area of the ceiling with richly fantastic painted decoration (figs. 54–57). Both works may be regarded as culminations of his easel painting.

The awakened idea of wall decoration led to the pursuit of still other techniques. For one thing, there was tapestry. In the 1960s Chagall supplied cartoons for no fewer than seven tapestries and closely supervised their working; among these were the three gigantic tapestries for the Parliament of Israel. There was also mosaic work. During the 1960s approximately six mosaics were completed, among them the outstanding 36-foot-wide *Odysseus* mosaic for Nice. Both these techniques involve the creation of a special area which interrupts the architectonic wall yet does not disturb the characteristics of the wall as surface. In the woven wall picture, the technique itself provides the appropriate surface, through the process of weaving. But with the mosaic, made up of small cubes of glass and colored stone embedded closely together, the play of light on the opaque or opalescent tesserae makes possible a shimmering and immaterial color effect over the surface plane that Chagall tirelessly sought in the colors of his paintings.

The inseparable interaction of light, color, and surface was precisely what the stained-glass window, by its very nature, has to offer. So it was natural that Chagall, because of the direction the painting of his later years was taking, found his way to the stained-glass window. Beginning in the late 1950s, he has made nearly fifty windows, some of huge dimensions.

Already in the summer of 1952 Chagall had intently studied the windows of Chartres Cathedral, and had been profoundly impressed by those prodigious walls of light, whose translucent

41 SONG OF SOLOMON I. 1957. Oil on canvas, 55⅛×64⅝″. *Collection the artist*

coloration transforms vast wall surfaces into the immaterial visionary field which he as a painter was trying by every means to achieve. He marveled at the free, abstract treatment of color and the delimitation of the surface by the irradiated color planes. The free play of figurative fantasy in those windows, with their abbreviated delineation of trees or animals and their fanciful and humorous marginalia, reminded him of his own inventions. With astonishment he became aware of the artistic freedom possible in this seemingly restrictive art form.

The small windows he did in the church at Assy were his first tentative experiment. But they led to an important commission in the course of which Chagall really began to understand and to develop the possibilities of stained glass This was for two windows for the ambulatory of Metz Cathedral;

the first window was completed in 1960. This was followed by a commission for windows in the cathedral of Rheims, and also for the small lancet windows in the choir of the Fraumünster in Zurich, which were completed in 1970. All of these commissions carried certain limitations with them: Chagall had to make his compositions fit into a Gothic structure and to make allowance for the neighboring windows already in existence.

But in June 1959, while he was still working on the first window for Metz, he received a wonderful commission. This was to do the stained glass in a self-contained sanctuary, a contemporary building which offered large undivided surfaces and all the freedom he could wish for. The Hadassah, an American organization of Zionist women's unions, had built a university clinic in the hills west of Jerusalem, and sug-

42 SAMSON DESTROYS THE TEMPLE. 1950. Ceramic, $12^3/_4 \times 11''$. *Private collection*

gested that Chagall decorate their synagogue with stained glass. The artist immediately agreed and left all other work aside. In only two years the work on the twelve big windows was finished, and in early 1962 the synagogue was consecrated.

The assignment appealed to Chagall's artistry in every respect. He had grown up in the intimate religious community of the Hasidic Jews of Vitebsk, had studied biblical subjects for more than thirty years, knew and loved Israel since his journeys of 1931, 1951, and 1957, and during the period of the persecution of the Jews and the years of war had reexperienced with deep emotion his sense of being a Jew and of belonging to Judaism. The task of adorning a holy place for Israel deeply touched his soul. "Always when I was at work," he states, "I felt as if Father and Mother were looking over my shoulder, and behind them were Jews, millions of other departed Jews of yesterday and thousands of years ago . . . ." What he sought to achieve he expressed in this way: "The synagogue shall be a crown for the Jewish queen and the windows the jewels of this crown . . . . The light of heaven is in these windows and by this means they are part of the good God." Even in the choice of color he referred to the instructions for making the breastplate of the high priests that were given by Moses in the book of Exodus.

One goes down a few steps into a rather dark room and there, above one, about twice the height of a man, is the radiant dome of light formed by the square lantern with sides about 26 feet long. Each side contains three rounded arches (11'1'' by 8'3''), and the windows are set into these. The lantern truly rests like a crown above the rectangular room, ringed by a narrow gallery, and fills it according to the position of the sun with the dominant color of the window illuminated by the sun. Each window has a dominant color following the contrasts of the color circle: blue, gold-yellow, red, and green.

The windows show the twelve tribes of Israel, deriving from the twelve sons of Jacob, whose characteristics are indicated in the blessings and prophecies of Jacob and Moses in the biblical text. One window is dedicated to each of the tribes. According to old Jewish tradition the portrayal of the human figure is forbidden, and consequently the iconographical content is limited to animals, fish, birds, plants, trees, implements, symbols, and Hebraic script signs. Chagall handled this iconographical inventory quite freely and was only generally influenced by the rather scant information of the biblical text.

Each window is like a flat landscaped area, into which, in heraldic abbreviation, have been placed the token objects symbolizing the individual tribes and their allotment within the prophecy. For the tribe of Reuben, which consisted of shepherds, sheep, fish, birds, and stars are depicted against a background of blue sea and sky, as symbols of the grandeur of nature. The tribe of Levi, which served in the temple and taught the Law, is characterized by the table of the Law sur-

43 DAVID WITH THE LYRE. 1951. Ceramic, $16^1/_2 \times 13^3/_4''$. *Private collection*

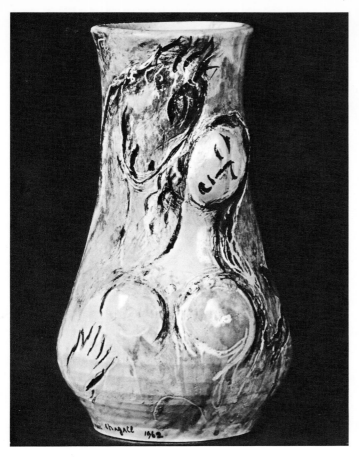

44 MIDSUMMER NIGHT'S DREAM. 1952. Ceramic, height 14⅞".
Private collection

45 THE BETROTHED. 1957. Ceramic, height 12½". *Private collection*

46 PEASANT AT THE WELL II. 1952. Ceramic, height 13". *Private collection*

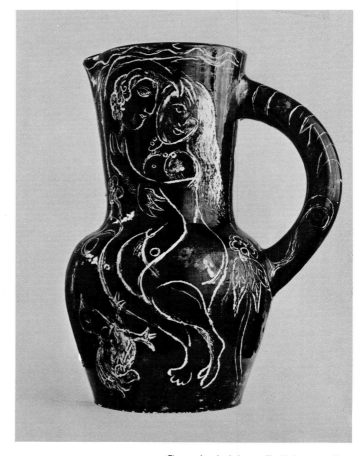

47 THE BLACK VASE. 1955. Ceramic, height 15". *Private collection*

48 NUDE. Undated. Marble sculpture, height 15¾". *Private collection*

49 PILLAR. 1953. Marble sculpture, 18⅞×9". *Private collection*

rounded by animals, and by the altar and candles, from which a golden light radiates through the whole window (fig. 53). The lion signifies the tribe of Judah, which furnished the political leaders; for the coast dwellers of the tribe of Zebulun a ship and two fish are depicted. The window for the peasant tribe of Issaker is filled out with vine branches, whose greenness lights up the whole field. War horses, lances, spears, and shields are the heraldic signs of the warrior tribe of Gad. The tribe of Benjamin, however, which Jacob in his prophetic valediction likened to a ravenous wolf—"In the morning he shall devour the prey, / And at night he shall divide the spoil"— is shown as the beast of prey before Jerusalem under a great rosette, above which appear two heraldic animals representing the other tribes of Israel. Around these fairly basic emblems Chagall has invented a wholly personal iconography. The Torah, the star of David, the seven-branched candelabrum, script signs, plants, and animals fill out the surfaces. They follow the associative play of fantasy and suggest various interpretations which stir the spectator's imagination. In his imagery Chagall has constantly sought the compact expressive power of the emblem, and in paintings such as *The Falling Angel* has indeed achieved this forceful symbolism. In the Jerusalem windows, however, because of the sacred nature of the task and the special character of stained glass, this emblematic art reaches its highest peak. Here the individual symbol becomes truly representative of a whole body of ideas.

Each window has a certain dominant color to produce an effect which Chagall also desired to achieve in the paintings of his later years—a kind of general tone, but with all the hues

50 COUPLE WITH BIRD. 1952. Marble relief, 12¼×12⅝". *Private collection*

and contrasts which derive from this tone combining to evoke a floating immaterial quality. The windows form four groups of three. The blue tonality is allotted to Reuben, Simeon, and Dan; the gold to Levi, Naphtali, and Joseph; the red to Judah, Zebulun, and (shining forth out of a blue ground) to Benjamin; the green to Issaker, Gad, and Asher. By the harmony of these individual dominating colors and the alternating em-

liberation in art roughly coincided with the establishment of
the state of Israel gives this happening historical as well as
intellectual significance.

The stained glass crowning the Hadassah synagogue is filled
with pictures of a deep inner joyfulness, which includes the
worship of love and all kinds of droll humor, such as we find
running so charmingly throughout Chagall's works. If we
consider his work as a whole, these windows stand as the
culmination of the painter's lifelong endeavors. They are walls
of light with that immaterial, supernatural further dimension,
built up entirely out of the relations of colored forms, which

51 LOVERS AND ANIMAL. 1957. Ceramic, height 12⅞″. *Private
collection*

52 THE VIRGIN AND CHILD. 1953. Bronze, height 26⅜″. *Private* ▶
collection

phasis on each according to the position of the sun, the room
is filled with a moving spiritual light. As in the case of his
painting of this period, Chagall has laid out his color in broad
areas, and has sought as far as possible to avoid the kaleidoscopic effect of glass mosaic, which the lattice system of the
lead strips tends to suggest. The lines of lead wander freely
over the surface and follow the contours of the color formations rather than the contours of the depicted objects. Because
of the importance for Chagall in achieving a tranquil expansion of color, he has put up with the resultant necessity for
a wide use of grisaille which here and there dulls the detail.

These windows can be shared by all men, regardless of
their religion. Nevertheless, it is in them that Judaism, tradi-
tionally ill-disposed toward pictures, is liberated into a new
pictorial expression. Mordecai Ardon, the Israeli painter and
a pupil of Paul Klee, once said that Jerusalem had gone
through life "as if with a sack over its head," while on
another shore of the Mediterranean stood radiant Athens,
ablaze with the glory of its pictures and statues, toward which
the envious Jerusalem had turned its blinded eyes. It seems
to me that in Chagall's synagogue windows a new relationship
of Jerusalem and Athens begins to materialize. That this

58   THE MESSAGE OF ODYSSEUS. 1967–68. Wall mosaic, 9′10″×36′. *Faculté de Droit et des Sciences Économiques de l'Université, Nice*

is an independent spiritual area paralleling the natural dimension.

Since the time of his encounter with Cézanne's work and Cubism in 1911–12, when he perceived the poetic significance of the independent Cubist space, Chagall directed his efforts as a painter toward preparing the picture surface as the field for the images from within his mind. Little by little the Cubist meshes fell away until there opened up a "further dimension" of the surface, free for every artistic discovery. This development obeyed the dictates of history. Manet and then Cézanne had reestablished the independent function of the picture surface, which had been lost since the Renaissance. Through Cézanne, perception of the evocative function of the surface had been introduced into twentieth-century painting, the ascertainment and elaboration of these evocative possibilities

being ascribed as its central task. The surface—both field and membrane—was the very place where the decisions were made concerning the visible image of painting, in accordance with twentieth-century perception. So much so, that Kurt Leonhard speaks of the "holy surface" in an essay of the same name, in which he examines the true function of the surface. If there is anywhere that this term, the holy surface, holds good, it must surely be in reference to Chagall's windows in the synagogue in Jerusalem.

Although obeying the decree of its historical period, Chagall's work nevertheless lies within it like a strangely timeless creation. Chagall always went his own way, and his individualism obliged him to make his life experiences into pictures. Certain of our modern critics, suffering from a sort of neurasthenic historical trendiness, unhesitatingly pick on the latest young

group as being representative of art as a whole and as the culmination of contemporary expression, and therefore accuse Chagall of not being "modern" and "contemporary." But if anyone were seriously to ask which work of art of the 1960s could in its scope and quality represent that period of history, then the answer would surely lie in the picture dome of the Hadassah synagogue.

Chagall belongs to the great picture makers of our time. It was he who filled the evocative picture, which stands at the center of the artistic endeavors of our century, with far-reaching poetic significance, and who initiated the pictorial use of metaphor which Surrealism was to develop in various directions. Max Ernst and Kurt Schwitters were both set on their paths by Chagall's influence. During my work on this book, Chagall slipped a note into my pocket. It was a short extract from the 1945 edition of André Breton's *Le Surréalisme et la peinture*. In it Breton, the spokesman of Surrealism, considers it a "deplorable omission that Chagall's contribution to the beginning of the movements of Dada and Surrealism has not been fully recognized," Chagall having been the first and only one to introduce pictorial metaphorism into modern painting. Breton then concludes with these words: "Nothing shows a more positive magic than this work, whose wonderful prismatic colors take up and transform the unrest of modern times and yet retain the old innocence by portraying what in nature is the principle of joyous delight—flowers and the expression of love." If we return once more to our starting point, we finally realize that it was precisely the power of his poetic perception that enabled Chagall to become the picture maker of our time, and without question a painter-poet.

41

59–63 Illustrations for *La Bible*, Paris: Tériade Éditeur, 1957. The etchings were made in 1936–39 (for Vollard) and 1952–56 (for Tériade). Measurements are 11–12½ × 8⅝–9½"

59   JACOB WEEPING FOR JOSEPH

60   JOSHUA

61   REBECCA AT THE WELL

62   LOT AND HIS DAUGHTERS

63   MOSES THROWING EGYPT INTO DARKNESS

64 MANILOV

65 THE CHARMING LADIES

66 THE PAINTERS

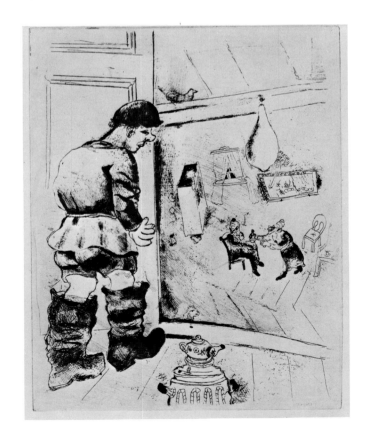

67 PROSCHKA

68 PLIOUCHKINE'S ROOM

69–72 Illustrations for the *Fables* of La Fontaine. La Fontaine, *Fables*, Paris: Tériade Editeur, 1952. The etchings were made in 1928–31 for Vollard. Measurements are 11⅜–12¼×9–9⅞″

69 THE WOLF, THE GOAT, AND THE KID

70 THE CART DRIVER STUCK IN THE MUD

71 THE LAUGHING MAN AND THE FISH

72 FORTUNA AND THE YOUNG BOY

Colorplates

Painted 1909–10

SELF-PORTRAIT WITH BRUSHES
(Autoportrait)

Oil on canvas, 22½ × 18⅞"
Collection Alport, Oxford, England

This is how the twenty-year-old Marc Chagall saw himself at the beginning of his career—every inch the "artist"! The picture proudly proclaims the self-conscious *"Anch'io sono pittore"*—"I also am a painter." Like the museum paintings of the Italian-Dutch school, the portrait is built up in broad outline, with the surface area filled in decoratively; the artist has his beret over his curly hair and the weapons of his trade like daggers in his hand. His attitude is characterized by naive delight in posing and in theatrical display, which was already evident in an earlier self-portrait, of 1908, showing him with a red half-mask in his hand. Here he regards the viewer with skepticism and an air of superiority. Except for the solid, formal buildup of the face from dark shadowy zones to warmly glowing light parts—which reveals a study of Rembrandt's portraits—and the skillful ornamental gradation from the silhouetted dark zone to the subdued light sections culminating in the eye-catching white of brushes, collar, and ornamentally stylized starflowers, the portrait would show nothing more than one of those "lads with curly hair and paintbox" who, as Bella recounts in her memoirs, made the young ladies of the middle-class Jewish intelligentsia in provincial Vitebsk feel a delicious thrill.

This kind of self-stylization seems completely at odds with the picture of a poor hallucinated youth, from a devout and impoverished small-town Jewish community in the Russian province, which Chagall sketched in his own autobiography and which has been constantly quoted ever since. Yet, the difference between the two images is not so great, for the portrait shows the twenty-year-old Chagall just at the point where he is about to break out of his early environment. As I have described in the text, Chagall had received quite a good education, in Vitebsk and later in St. Petersburg. On coming home to Vitebsk for summer vacations—as, for instance, in 1909 when he began painting this *Self-Portrait*—he might well have felt himself an "artist" in this provincial milieu, for he was regarded as being such an exceptional personage.

The small, somewhat exalted circle of young Russian intellectuals, painters, poets, and young ladies from good bourgeois homes who were studying in Moscow or St. Petersburg—among them Chagall's future wife Bella—provided the right background for his self-confirmation. Bella heard it whispered that the young painter was so poor he had to paint his pictures

"on the stove among the chickens." Such not altogether accurate little tales melted the girls' hearts. They wanted to help their painter and secretly even modeled for him; these were quite innocent proceedings, but nevertheless gave them the feeling of being self-reliant, emancipated young women. There was a good deal of play-acting, and many a theatrical personification and self-stylization was carried over into real life.

Chagall certainly did not paint his pictures "on the stove." While in Vitebsk, he lodged at a gendarme's house where he had rented a little room all to himself which served him as a studio. Here—and often in Bella's company—he dreamed his first dreams of his future life as an artist. It was here that the *Self-Portrait* was made, together with the life-size, half-length portrait of his sister Aniuta and the celebrated portrait of Bella, *My Fiancée in Black Gloves*, of 1909. All these show a decorative treatment of the surface and the desire to achieve something solid, like the art of the museums.

Chagall's *Self-Portrait* is certainly less important as an artistic production than as a psychological self-revelation at the beginning of his career. It shows an artist who, in depicting his own physiognomy, seems almost to stress a certain mocking "arrogance" which in a young artist is the hallmark of his freedom and which soon enabled Chagall to juggle freely the requirements of reality and, when it suited his poetic fancy or his spirit of contradiction, to turn everything topsy-turvy. The theatricals too had their deeper meaning, in the desire to transform reality into a counterworld of heightened poetic fantasy, which—as in the theater or the circus—had to be staged by appropriate means. Thus we see before us someone quite different from a modest, dreamy ghetto painter deeply impressed by Hasidic religious doctrine. Chagall has always tried to get away from this legend, although naturally there is a grain of truth in it. If right from the start he underlined his *"Anch'io sono pittore!"* so emphatically, it was with the consciousness which guided him throughout his whole life as a painter—that all things meaningful, poetic, or religious can only count as a "picture" when the impulses derived from emotion and experience are converted into painting. Chagall liked to call this transformation process the "chemistry" of painting, and he worked on this all his life. For this reason he needed to be aware of his own mission as an artist.

Painted 1910

STILL LIFE WITH LAMP
(Nature morte à la lampe)

Oil on canvas, 31⅞ × 17¾″
Galerie Rosengart, Lucerne

Chagall had left Russia in August 1910, and this picture was painted later that year in Paris. On a small allowance provided by a St. Petersburg benefactor, he was at last able to live as a free painter in the city which to his mind had seemed the Mecca of painting ever since his studies with Bakst, who had already acquainted him with the new developments in French painting, and had directed his attention to Gauguin, Van Gogh, and Matisse.

The still life here belongs to one of the first groups of Parisian paintings. It demonstrates a new *éclat* of color and a new approach to surface, which the painter began to envisage as a bed for the development of decorative color arrangements rather than a field for sustaining illusionist perspective. The color explores the full range of the spectrum: the general tonality, consisting of the adjacent tones of brown through orange into pure yellow, responds to the blue color passages emerging from the dark zones. Where the gradation of color-light demands a red, the complementary green also appears. These color movements make their way across the surface in the form of an uneasy, lurching ornamentation of a rather Oriental character. The various objects, such as the fruit bowl or the lamp, are pressed into this ornamental surface arrangement without regard for optical probability or solidity. From this array of colors emanates a powerful light, distributed in circular shapes over the surface and culminating in the lamp—or exploding, one might say, for the color is laid on as violently as if "the tubes of paint were sticks of dynamite, bursting with light," as the young Derain described his own feeling for color at about the same time.

In fact, there is nothing to stop us from connecting this new explosive color in Chagall's work with the color revolt of the Fauves. Yet the construction and the emotional fullness of the color arrangement bring another name to mind—that of Gauguin. The building up of color-light from adjoining colors, which Gauguin called "the production of a color-tone with the help of all variations of this tone," alone is enough to make us think of Gauguin. But, in addition, the *"gaucherie,"* as Gauguin called it—the characteristically awkward drawing of the figures and objects, whose crude contours fit more expressively into the ornamental color arrangement than an objectively "correct" rendering would—and particularly the poetic, emotional fullness of color, which Gauguin liked to call "enigmatic color," make the connection between the two

artists complete. It was Gauguin who, above and beyond the constructive handling of free color, so important to Cézanne and later to Matisse, desired to achieve something far more abstract and sublimely poetic—the revelation of the mythical background to reality in painting. And that was exactly what Chagall, until then unconsciously, felt he wanted to do. It was along Gauguin's lines that he began to develop his personal "chemistry."

In spite of the unmistakable French influence, the coloring is very personal and has a visionary ardor about it that is more Russian than French, having that peculiarly mystic quality we know from Russian folklore and also from the pictures of the early Kandinsky or Jawlensky. This is in accord with the unusual subject matter. The theme is not a French, but a Russian, interior. The focal point is the lighted petroleum lamp, that wondrous object which used to shed an atmosphere of cheer and coziness over family gatherings in the evening; it held such a firm position in Chagall's mental inventory that it turns up time and again in his work as the emblem of peace and domesticity. It has nothing less than a personal character: like a being in its own right, with a personal poetic claim on existence, it dominates the picture space and summons up the two attendant figures, Russian country people, whom we may suppose to be the artist's father and mother. Thus the theme has been conjured up out of dreamy, musing memory by the play of evocative colors.

During the years in Paris, despite his love for that city, Chagall was homesick for Vitebsk. His fantasy was full of the pictures of his childhood, which in memory were transfigured into a poetic dream reality. In the milieu of a Western capital, there seemed something exotic about his ideas, which soon made people think of him as a teller of tales and legends, a notion which persists even today. But in fact he was confronted by the same problem which faced French painting in those years: how the recognized or sensed "harmonic" or "mythic" background to reality could be pictorially expressed, how the colored surface could become the mirror of a psychically experienced fuller reality, how a poetic dream could be painted. Because the Parisian school from Cézanne to the Fauves and the Cubists had been working on this same problem with great logic, it was from them that Chagall could gain the most helpful encouragement.

Painted 1911–12

I AND THE VILLAGE
(Moi et le village)

Oil on canvas, 75¼×59¼"
Museum of Modern Art, New York City. Mrs. Simon Guggen-heim Fund

A clear example of how Chagall turned the picture plane into the mirror of memory is given in the large painting *I and the Village*. The surface itself has a "mirror-like" quality. Without any impasto, the spontaneous brushwork gives a painting that is shiny and smooth, suggesting the transparent hardness that is produced by the technique of painting on glass. Behind this glassy exterior the picture world unfolds in a further dimension. As in a painting on glass, the surface area is folded in flat layers parallel to the picture plane, in the manner of a relief. This basic structure of the picture space is many-faceted: here the areas are small and arranged in a decorative pattern; there in empty contrasted fields; here in luminous transparent planes; there fitted together in interpenetrating segments. Merely out of these superimposed layers is created a crystalline spatial structure, a backwards-and-forwards rhythm, which gives the impression of a breathing surface that nonetheless retains its character as a plane. The pictorial space created in this way has nothing in common with the perspective of the three-dimensional natural world which surrounds us. It is a completely independent pictorial space, brought into being only by paint and brush.

It is based on a refined geometry which strictly governs the surface ornament. Along the central perpendicular—and somewhat below midpoint in order to have a firm center of gravity—a large circle can be seen which seems to hang in the crosslines of the diagonals. These, it is true, exist only as imaginary guidelines, but so many other lines—straight, curving, or undulating—take them up, allude to them, or toy with them that they are still quite clearly recognizable in the crisscross diagonal movements. In contrast to the concentrical calm of the circle, in which the diagonals are refracted as in a glass ball, the leaping, playful, diagonal offshoots bring in many richly contrasted movements. This geometrical net binds the whole construction firmly inside the picture rectangle so that, although in many places the edges of the picture cut through objective details, these do not point outside the picture margins but remain structural elements of the internal design. Nothing projects outside the self-contained unity of the ornamental surface.

This independent field is illuminated by independently used color, which disregards local, or objective, description. It runs the whole gamut of the color scale, varying the dominant green-red contrast with gentler color passages ranging from blue to the sparingly used yellow. These basic colors are given radiance by the addition of the so-called non-colors—white and black—as is clearly evident in the magically colorful mosaic of little houses on a black ground or in the blazing red of the

circle segment whose bright heat is kindled by the adjacent paths of white. Since the colors are in tone groupings—which allows the individual color to be effective only as part of the ensemble—color loses its material quality and becomes the bearer of an independent, immaterial color-light. This light has nothing to do with natural illumination issuing from a specific source of light; it is a pure inner picture light, created out of the light values of the individual colors and their interaction. It is split into facets in the spatial and ornamental network of the picture structure, and shines unorientated out of the entire surface of the painting. The color alone is the source of all light. Immaterial, without limitations, floating and transparent, antinatural, it conforms to the crystal structure of the plane and irradiates it with a magical glow.

This surface field, produced by pictorial means alone, is the perfect playground for free ideas; its crystalline, radiant structure is capable of reflecting and refracting every vision of the imagination. It is the pictorial response to the realization that reality, as revealed by the poetic power of memory, is made up of manifold superimposed images creating a composite and simultaneous field of experience. This cannot possibly be expressed in all its fullness by a static and perspectival pictorial presentation. The new and entirely transformed surface field, however, represents this remembered reality. It does not reproduce any visible view, but represents, materializes, evokes images emerging from the less conscious regions, which shape and perfect themselves into a picture of memory only during the actual process of painting.

This fascinating surface pattern is energized by the hallucinatory contents of the picture. At the right, solidly positioned in the constructive framework, appears the sliced-off, greenly illuminated profile of a man, an abridged version of the painter's own face. In amazement he stares fixedly at a white cow's head, which emerges from the light-blue-and-white layer of the crystalline, fragmented plane like an apparition from a dream and stares back at the painter. Their intimate relationship is indicated by the fine line which connects the two eyes so steadfastly regarding each other. It is further emphasized by the shy gesture with which the beringed hand introduces a wonderfully elaborate, glittering nosegay like a love token into the symbolic world of the picture. The cow! Chagall recalls, "The cow in our yard, with her milk as white as snow, the cow who used to talk to us." In the magical atmosphere of the picture the cow loses her animal status and becomes a familiar personality, symbolic of rural security, of the mother, of woman, of the beloved even; the glittering nosegay is meant for her. Additional symbolic objects set the scene: at the top is a naively abbreviated version of a typical Russian village with its domed church, out of which the priest is solemnly peeping; a peasant with his scythe strides across the open field; a peasant woman points out the way for him, and the fact that she, together with some of the little houses, is upside down is not the least disturbing in this dream atmosphere, for she only serves as a symbolic sign in the poetic context of the picture; in the transparent region where the cow's head appears, a milkmaid sits and milks the same white cow. All these elements, fitted like allusive words into the rhythmic construction of the picture, call up a whole sequence of meanings. So, out of Chagall's longing memory of his native Vitebsk slowly emerges a readable picture which reveals the entire complexity of the poetically transfigured memory picture. It is no "view," no rebus pieced together with symbols, but an *imago* which reflects the psychically experienced reality in the pictorial parable of colored forms.

Painted 1911–12

THE DRUNKARD
(Le saoul)

Oil on canvas, 33½ × 45¼″
Collection Frau Milada Neumann, Caracas

The Drunkard was painted·a few months before the completion of *I and the Village* (colorplate 3). It was among the first paintings Chagall exhibited at the Paris Salon des Indépendants, which opened on March 20, 1912. So, presumably, it was made at the turn of 1911–12, and this agrees with the date Chagall has given it.

It was preceded by a small gouache, made while Chagall was working on a series of interiors showing a single figure near a table—small sketches in which the tranquillity of the room forms an emotional contrast to the uneasy agitation of the human figure. This gouache shows a comparatively realistic view of an interior with a table and two chairs, with the drinker on the right-hand side. Chagall's strange invention of the detached head trying to reach the floating bottle is already to be found here. On the table are playing cards, a bowl of fruit, and a herring. A window in the back wall looks out on a country scene, and a cow is stretching her head through the window. The variety of detail in the description of the room gives the picture a certain anecdotal character.

In the oil version shown here, however, the anecdotal features have been largely blotted out. The interior view with back wall, window, and peering cow has given way to an abstract plane structured by a pattern of large rhomboids. The inventory of objects has been reduced to a few stylized items which lie flattened on the plane, although retaining their characteristic contours. The reversed perspective of the table also fits into the surface ornamentation. The whole canvas, with its ornamental arrangement and slightly agitated spatial construction, is lit up by a magic color-light which streams out of the entire surface area. It derives its power from the fundamental contrasts of blue and yellow, and of red and green, which are accompanied by a profusion of passages of colors neighboring each other in the spectrum: from yellow through orange to red, from orange to green-yellow, and from red-violet to blue. These graduations of color interact to generate the unreal light. Once more, as in *I and the Village*, the radiant, ornamental, independent surface area becomes the field for the various details. *The Drunkard* contains the same construction of the evocative surface as the mirror of the psychically experienced and poetically enhanced reality which was carried through to perfection in *I and the Village*.

The theme is evoked by the few sparse objective details which stand like isolated accents in the rhythmic composition. On the left is the calm zone of things—the table with the culinary tokens of fish, fowl, and bowl; on the right, agitated by diagonals, is the aggressive zone of the neurotic human being, with the knife as a symbol of this aggression. Parallel to the man is the floating bottle and the man's own head, detached from his body and freely hovering; it is absolutely right as far as compositional arrangement is concerned. As to the motif, the alogical, absurd, and astonishing displacement makes the unreality of the entire scene crystal clear. In those days Chagall was constantly preoccupied with the theme of a calm interior and its peaceful things disturbed by the passion of the neurotically agitated human being, that "disturber of the universe," as man always appears in Chagall's picture world. Thus *The Drunkard* was created in response to this general poetic idea. It too is an *imago* brought to completeness—not a view, not a symbolic arrangement, but rather a poetic sentence written in hieroglyphs, which gains powerful expression by pictorial means.

In the Salon des Indépendants the picture quite rightly hung next to paintings by the Cubists and artists of related styles. In its colorful structure, which emphasizes the independent light values of color, it clearly shows the influence of Delaunay, with whom Chagall was friendly during his first Parisian years, and in its underlying geometric basic pattern it shows the influence of the artists of the Section d'Or. The formal architecture of the plane is based on inventions of the Cubists. Chagall detached himself from classical Cubism and its analytical method from the outset, because he felt it was "too naturalistic." He had more in common with the artists of the secret Cubist secession for which Apollinaire invented the term Orphism. This group included Léger, Delaunay, Gleizes, De La Fresnaye, Le Fauconnier, Villon, and Metzinger, among others—a broad phalanx of artists. There Chagall found what he was looking for—the free exercise of bright color, which Analytical Cubism, with its severe concentration on form, had reduced to gray and brown. He also found there a greater receptivity to poetic expression, from which the strict adherents of Analytical Cubism had held aloof. It was the general intellectual climate and the ideas circulating among his friends about a way of painting which, like music or poetry, could arrive at an extended and poetically enhanced interpretation of reality—even though this lay beyond the visual sphere—which he found helpful to his own development. So he took up suggestions here and there, even from lesser artists such as Le Fauconnier, which could aid him to realize his conception of the picture surface as a shining prism capable of reflecting not only the poetic sensations of reality and memory, but also the free projections of a fantasy exploring mythical and cosmic realms. In fact, Chagall's pictures, in their poetic range, stand out quite distinctly from the circle of Orphist paintings. Not until much later was Surrealism to open up the source from which Chagall's pictorial poetry derives its nourishment—the dream, memory, and the images of the unconscious.

Painted 1911–12

TO RUSSIA, ASSES, AND OTHERS
(A la Russie, aux ânes et aux autres)

Oil on canvas, 61⅜×48"
Musée National d'Art Moderne, Paris

What strangely surrealistic dreams of a distant reality still alive in memory the picture surface can reflect is shown by this painting. It was one of the first pictures made in Chagall's new studio in La Ruche, which was big enough to allow him to make larger compositions than before. It must therefore have been painted at the beginning of 1912—contrary to the date which was later inserted—but it goes back to a small watercolor of the previous year. Together with *The Drunkard* (colorplate 4), it was exhibited at the Salon des Indépendants in March 1912.

This picture must have been regarded as an extremely strange and exotic intruder there. Indeed, it was unique among French paintings of that time, not only because of its content, which seemed so naively extravagant to French eyes, but also because of its magical color, radiantly emerging from a dark ground. Thus the critics of the day did not speak of Chagall as a richly inventive painter making pictures out of dreams and the unconscious—that was left to the Surrealists to discover—but, like Canudo in 1913, spoke of him as one of the "most amazing colorists among the new painters."

The surface field in this painting is again divided into flat, faceted layers and is illuminated by the brilliance of the colors themselves. This "evocative surface," as I have called it, again shows objects and figures in their characteristic outline, which fits in with the surface ornamentation, and again we feel transported into an enchanted, anaturalistic dimension, which earlier I compared with the effect of painting on glass. A sensitive eye can still faintly discern the basic geometric pattern of the ornamentation, built up of squares and crossing diagonals. Although veiled by many divergent movements and covered by color, it is like an underlying field of force supporting the constellation of appearances in the picture and holding it in a floating equilibrium.

The vision emerging from the picture plane is highly surprising. It unfolds in a sphere which is completely out of this world, where the rules of logic, gravity, probability, and normality do not count any more. Indeed, they are directly reversed and as a result reveal something wondrous yet natural and inevitable as in dream pictures. Looking like a messenger of the gods in her peacock robe, a milkmaid with a pail hurries through the magically illuminated heavenly zone down to a red cow which stands quietly feeding, while suckling a calf and a child, on the rooftops of a village. This bewildering contrast of the byre-warm country scene and the cosmic zone,

irradiated by astral light prisms or mysteriously sinking into darkness, pushes the earthly things into a new kind of surrealistic dimension in which it does not seem unusual for a milkmaid to appear as a new constellation against the background of the night sky. It is precisely that inconsequence of circumstances, that constant interchange of reality and possibility with the improbable, which causes the chain of logic governing our concept of the outer world suddenly to break and makes the unreal appear as a poetic perception of reality—in this case as the poetic essence of a remembered reality. The contrast between the real and the unreal causes objective reality to appear as miraculous.

A comparison of the oil painting with the small watercolor sketch gives us an idea of how this vision came about and how the transformation of the real to the unreal was accomplished. The sketch shows a sloping hill pasture in which stands the cow with her two young ones, while the milkmaid comes striding down with her pail. If it were not for her detached head and for a large magical constellation in the sky, this scene could be taken as a naive childhood memory picture of life in rural Vitebsk. But once at work on the large picture, and in tense anticipation of what would be achieved in it, the painter pushed this commonplace reality more and more into the realm of the unreal: the cow ends up on the roofs of the sleeping Russian fairy-tale village and becomes a gigantic, good-natured, all-providing idol, nourishing animal and human being alike; the robust country girl becomes a hurrying light-footed messenger whose head gets left behind while marveling at the astral lights blazing in the vault of heaven; the dark background, fired by magical colors, becomes the cosmic sphere where all miracles are possible. What is produced in the end is a pictorial metaphor entirely removed from reality—a parable which transfigures the picture of memory into poetry.

The pictorial metaphor is created only by an inspired association of colored forms. This was the reason why the preparation of the picture plane as a field capable of supporting the images was of paramount importance. As for the contents and meaning of the picture, these were crystallized in the colored forms and could no longer be described in words by the painter.

The strange title comes from Chagall's poet friend, Blaise Cendrars. The dedication—which is what it amounts to—appealed to Chagall, so he accepted this droll and cryptic title.

Painted 1911–12

THE HOLY COACHMAN
(Le saint voiturier)

Oil on canvas, 58¼ × 46¼"
Private collection

Once Chagall had found the appropriate means of expression, the most remarkable pictures followed. The richer and freer his painting became the stronger grew his visionary faculties, and he willingly submitted to the stream of pictures flowing from the unconscious.

They were all associated with Vitebsk and formed an unbroken bond between him and his recollections of the distant land of childhood. He felt completely uninhibited in his inspired fantasy. His memories included all kinds of droll, grotesque, and absurd incidents which he did not hesitate to include, and indeed his peculiar brand of puckish humor liked to emphasize farcical and absurd aspects. His creations were never intended to be frightening, but were meant to lure out of reality its wondrous, fantastic, and droll elements—that mythical and secret realm Shakespeare displayed so perfectly in *A Midsummer Night's Dream*. The shock given by the absurd was meant to break through the meshes of logic which limit our perception of reality and to create a pure astonishment at what the real can offer—if for once one tries to stand it on its head. Chagall sometimes provoked such breaks in the logical pattern purposely, or, if they occurred fortuitously, he accepted them to keep his mind open to all sensations and the amazement which is the richest source of poetic awareness.

One of the most remarkable examples is *The Holy Coachman*. It was painted shortly after *To Russia, Asses, and Others* (colorplate 5) and shows similar formal characteristics. The color, however, is more richly modulated. Strident color values are suppressed; instead a muted white, olive green, and dark ochre sound the basic harmony, and are complemented by a deep blue and a heightened sharp red. This more subdued modulation broadens the coloristic experiment which began with the loud and naive color scheme of *The Drunkard* (colorplate 4).

Once again the title comes from Blaise Cendrars, but is not readily understandable when we first look at the figure hurtling down and sliding like a sledge across the snowy field, even if the little flaming coronet—the Jewish prayer cap—on the messenger's head, together with the domed church, suggests something holy. However—the picture is upside down! At the Berlin exhibition of 1914 Herwarth Walden, following some impulse, hung the picture the wrong way up; Chagall, struck by the unexpected apparition of this profane angel bursting upon the scene, accepted the inversion just as he had accepted Cendrars' verbal metaphor, and from then on kept it this way. Such a reversal, however, was a familiar occurrence in his work. He worked at his pictures from all angles; either way up, one of the houses in the background is always upside down.

If we reverse the picture the motif becomes readable in Cendrars' sense. Chagall had a similar theme in mind in a small oil painting he made in 1917. In the painting here, if seen in its original position, the red-orange plane becomes a seat, the angelic youth a young man who, seized by some devout thought perhaps suggested by the scroll upon his knees, is bent backward as if by some supernatural power so that his holy coronet touches the foot of the house of God. If one also bears in mind that the tightly bent bow of the body and the dynamic shapes which support its direction seem to be speedily moving the hallucinated figure toward the left, one can grasp the association which led Cendrars to choose his strange title, which does indeed correspond to the metaphoric aspects of the picture. The fact that Chagall could think of nothing to write on the scroll which had so mightily inspired the youth except his own name and that of Paris, although a word from any psalm would have served, is one of those teasing puzzles the painter likes to put in when the spectator's desire for interpretation threatens to lead him into overly esoteric regions.

Yet the inversion of the picture has very little to do with riddles of this kind. If we reverse the picture again we are struck by its rare visionary power, like a chance enlightenment. The inspired reader is still there, but now he plunges headlong into the coldness of the world like a tempestuous young prophet, with the holy scroll fluttering behind him, while the flames of his coronet reach over to the sign of the church, where the Law is kept safe. Unexpectedly, a stirring pictorial metaphor has come into being, alluding to the believer's mission in the world, for he is often able to kindle the godly spark hidden in the things of this world by the force of his inspiration. Chagall's entire artistic work, which includes irony and clowning, is unswervingly directed toward the discovery of such pictorial metaphors, inexpressible in words.

Painted 1911–12

HOMAGE TO APOLLINAIRE
(Hommage à Apollinaire)

Oil on canvas, 82¼×78"
Stedelijk van Abbemuseum, Eindhoven

In the same period he painted *The Holy Coachman* (colorplate 6) Chagall painted this large canvas, which he dedicated to Apollinaire in 1913 after a visit by the poet to his studio. It is the most esoteric picture symbol ever made by Chagall, and its composition is a paradigm of his newly found picture structure.

The motif, expressed in abstract formal movements, is not easily recognizable at first glance. Some previous watercolors and drawings, however, show that in those days Chagall had the theme of the first man and woman, Adam and Eve, very much in mind. At first he represented the subject relatively naturalistically, in the Garden of Eden, complete with snake and apple; later he conceived the motif in more and more abstract terms, and sought to bind it into a great coherent design of a spiral flowing into a circle. The painting *Homage to Apollinaire* shows the results of this endeavor. The theme has been pared down to its essential and universal elements, the paradisiacal scenery has disappeared, and only the apple, symbol of the Fall, remains.

The human couple, standing straight and tall in the center like the hand of a clock, is a symbolic abbreviation of the Genesis legend of the creation of woman from the rib of Adam; the lower parts of their bodies are still joined, and part at the genital zone. This point, where the sexes unfold, is not only the place of intersection for the diagonals on which the whole construction is based, but also the beginning of the spiral which slowly rotates outward and eventually finishes in a circle. This circle, which faces the viewer like the dial of a tower clock and alludes to the universe of man geared to the rhythm of time, is surrounded by infinite space, which is indicated by cloud formations, the midnight blue of the sky, and the stellar hemisphere at the upper left. Against this background of infinity looms the time-governed universe, for with the Fall man was no longer part of the timelessness of the eternal. With the partition of the sexes also began the succession of the generations, punctuated, like the flow of time in the ticking of a clock, by birth and death. The symbol of the clock was constantly on Chagall's mind; in the upward-sweeping arc of red he strikes the hours: nine! ten! eleven!—and where the twelfth hour is supposed to strike he writes his own name—once completely, another time without vowels, and then his forename in Roman and Hebrew characters. In order to make the metaphor not too clear, and to satisfy his natural sense of mystification, Chagall omits the first digit of the ten, while in the eleven he gives it the appearance of a casual brushstroke.

Was this pictorial metaphor preconceived in the painter's mind when he began work? Not entirely, in my opinion. I believe it was the formal invention of the growing spiral and the unfolding of color in its wake which suggested the symbolic form to him. Form and content are not easily separable here; a hint suggested by a color sequence can quite unexpectedly awaken awareness of the symbolic attributes of a form.

The color is handled very curiously indeed. The bright colors are pushed back, and a subdued tone like the note of a gong comes out of the accord of colors. Its metallic resonance is enhanced by the use of gold and silver colors, adorning the plane with heraldic solidity. The optical effect is somewhat surprising. From under the silver emerges the curving band of red, seeming to move upward and, urged on by the inner tongue-shaped red portion, past the numerals until it is submerged beneath the gold. At the top lies a section of passive dark green, but this seems to pass across the dark segment of brown-violet toward the truncated arc of blue. This movement is overtaken by the gold, which reappears in the segment at the upper right as the continuation of the gold portion in the dial.

The sequence of colors, in conjunction with the dynamic forms, makes it seem as if the whole colored construction is slowly rotating in a clockwise direction. This sense of rotation not only emphasizes the symbolic portrayal of the flow of time but seems to make the idea truly evident by means of color alone.

Thoughts about the possibilities of color expressing movement were very much in the air at the time. The Neo-Impressionists had already had a notion of it, and then the Futurists activated the newly discovered mobile tendencies of colored forms and used them to express their concept of "universal dynamism." Within Chagall's circle it was Delaunay who frequently occupied himself with the *"sens giratoire,"* the sense of rotation in color. Chagall certainly adapted the theoretical knowledge of Delaunay's more abstract formalism to suit his poetic use of metaphor, but he always had an instinctive fear of logical theories.

In the lower left is his declaration of devotion to the poets, written around the naive emblem of a heart pierced by an arrow, which was not put in until 1914. There we find Blaise Cendrars, and then Canudo, who often used to visit Chagall in his studio. Next comes the name of Apollinaire, with whom he became friendly in 1913. Finally there is the name of Herwarth Walden, whom he came to know in 1913 through Apollinaire. The name of a painter does not appear.

Painted 1911–12

MAZIN, THE POET
(Le poète Mazin)

Oil on canvas, 28¾ × 21¼"
Collection Frau Ida Meyer-Chagall, Basel

The poet Mazin was one of Chagall's friends. His anxious face with its protuberant forehead is also portrayed in a sketch which is still in Chagall's cabinet of drawings. Mazin lived in La Ruche and often called on Chagall when passing by; he used to sit in his corner, grateful for a cup of coffee. Chagall has painted him like that, shyly sitting at the table sipping his coffee, with a melancholy face and a great dome of a forehead; the book on his knees is the attribute of his profession.

La Ruche, a collection of neglected and very cheap studios in the vicinity of the Vaugirard slaughterhouses, was the haunt of the bohemians of Paris, among them, as poorest of the poor, a whole group of immigrants, including Russians. Chagall still recalls with amusement how the occasional smell of fried liver, the only meal he knew how to cook, used to attract all kinds of hungry visitors, among them his bitterly poor countryman Soutine and quiet neighbors like Mazin.

Chagall did not lead much of a social life at his studio. On Friday evenings he saw many of the young artists at Canudo's, and occasionally he was the guest of Robert and Sonia Delaunay. He worked mostly at night, and recalls how, seized by work fever, he finished painting the vast canvas *Dedicated to My Fiancée* (fig. 18) in the dark, because his oil lamp had gone out while he was working. His personal contacts were many and varied: his friend Blaise Cendrars always stopped in when passing, read his poems to him, and marveled at the poetic dreams of his painter friend; Canudo, who was a friend of Marinetti's, the pope of the Futurists, came to see his new paintings; Max Jacob appeared on the scene; and then in 1913 Apollinaire, the "gentle Zeus" of the artistic avant-garde, visited him. Much of the atmosphere of the magician's workshop in Chagall's studio has gone into the poems dedicated to him by Cendrars and Apollinaire, including something of his way of working, using evocative realistic details to represent a whole complex of meanings. Also his fellow countrymen turned up: there was the great Bakst, who created the settings for Diaghilev's famous theater and who even asked to be painted by Chagall; occasionally the deputy and politician Max Moisevitch Vinaver, who had given Chagall an allowance upon his arrival in Paris from St. Petersburg; and Lunacharsky, who later became People's Commissar for Culture but at that time was a political writer and lived in La Ruche. Although Lunacharsky could not make much of Chagall's pictures, he nevertheless helped him considerably during the first years after the Revolution. But these were exceptional cases. The people who dropped in during the everyday course of life were mainly the poor devils of La Ruche, among them Mazin.

The portrait is most likely a product of chance, brought about by the touching sight of the poet sitting so forlornly at the table. Portraits were not of much interest to Chagall in those days; he had even declined to paint Bakst. Clearly they were too close to reality for him, which is one reason why the motifs of his Paris wanderings so seldom found their way into his painting. But this figure had something of a poetic background. By no means intended as a finished portrait, the picture has a sketchiness that tries to seek out that poetic background. The poet has been placed close to the edge of the picture, and the aggressive-looking white table corner with the austere frame above it seems to push him even farther into his corner. He retreats into the dark color zone of the brown and red as if into a niche. Only the white forehead, the multicolored book, and the responding areas of white in the clothes seem to counteract the meditative mood. Even though Chagall's intention was to capture the immediate impression of the man sitting there timidly, lost in daydreams, there is, at a less conscious level, a determined desire for solid form in the organization of the picture. The skillfully distributed white values make up a well-balanced surface ornamentation and at the same time establish the spatial construction of the pictorial design. The strong color accents of the book and the trousers and the row of light-red fingers on the right hand are linked with the array of varied colors on the bottle. A net of connected forms and colors has been spread across the picture.

Painted 1911–12

THE POET, or HALF-PAST THREE
(Le poète, ou Half-Past Three)

Oil on canvas, 77⅝ × 57½″
Philadelphia Museum of Art. Louise and Walter Arensberg
Collection

What Chagall was aiming at in meaning and form in the little portrait study of Mazin is made surprisingly evident by *The Poet*, a large composition which he felt obliged to carry out with precision. In the basic features of the composition and the buildup of the figure it follows the Mazin portrait study, but in the construction of the plane, the transparency of forms, and the fragmented analysis of the material things depicted, it is totally different. It is as though the artist, proceeding from the suggestions which occurred to him while painting the portrait, had stripped the skin off the natural motif and deliberately exposed the underlying construction. The picture was certainly painted at a somewhat later date than the portrait of Mazin, presumably in the summer of 1912 and in the wake of *I and the Village* (colorplate 3), with which it has in common not only its size but also its character as a *tableau manifeste*.

It is, in fact, a kind of exemplar in which the painter has again gone through all the impulses which had come his way from Cubism, Futurism, and the Section d'Or, in order to arrive at a paradigm of the new picture structure taken to its furthest—and for Chagall, quite unusual—consequence.

Even more emphatically than *I and the Village* the picture now becomes quite flat. The white ground does nothing but stress the surface, which is given only a very slight effect of spatial movement by the faint gradations of gray and the geometrical pattern work. It seems solid as a wall, but loses its materiality through the transparency of the fine planes and the crystalline structure they create. On this picture surface, pulled tight like a flexible membrane, lie the depicted objects, themselves also transparent and faceted like crystals, as if ironed onto the flat ground.

The color holds the fragmented figurative forms together in groups. The basic harmony is provided by an active red which rules the table zone and a meditative blue which is given to the figure. The active red corresponds to the dynamic mobility of the diagonals, which bring the whole right-hand side, including the individual objects, into stormy motion. The knife rolls between the two spherical objects on the table as if on ball bearings; the fork worms its way upward, in a perfect example of Futurist movement theory; and the bottle jumps out of the perpendicular and zooms away like a bullet. At the top right the red movement explodes in a scattered pattern of small shapes. This is actually the design on a curtain, but in the formal context seems like a slow-motion vortex of forms blown in by the wind. Only the elegant little still life of the delicate drinking glass and the accurately folded paper remains in a vertical position, but by its fragile though stable character makes us doubly aware of the commotion all around.

The turbulent red zone is countered by the well-shaped, perpendicular tower of the blue. The tranquil eurhythmy of the posture—with the arm which guides the pencil parallel to the bent arm which holds the cup—emphasizes the solid rhythmic stature of the blue figure, which, because of its transparent architecture and the spiritual character of its color, takes on something of a solemn and meditative air.

The way the green is used is very curious. This color is used for the head crowning the blue figure, and is repeated in the cat and in the ball on the table. Wherever it appears, it is used to create a plastic quality, in marked contrast to the general flatness of the construction. The vertex of the green accents is the head, which through its modeling looks like a strange globe floating upwards. The effect is made more striking by the fact that the pointed, dynamic red section is aimed in the direction of the complementary green, and even stranger because the head has been twisted around so that it no longer sits on the neck. Like a spinning globe, it seems to have turned itself upwards, impelled by the storm sweeping in from the right, and to be watching the light circular forms which repeat its rotating movement, delicately floating and fading away above.

This description has mainly focused on the formal elements, yet has already touched on the contents. What has been delineated here on the evocative surface as a complex picture is precisely what was an underlying possibility in the sketch from nature of the poet Mazin. It is an exclusively pictorial metaphor, detached from all references to reality, of the poetic man during the stormy invasion of inspiration, who, hallucinating and beside himself, ponders his dreams and rhythmic cadences—at the weird hour of half past three in the morning, as the title of the picture tells us.

Yet too much stress should not be laid on the contents of the picture. What mattered above all at this point to Chagall was the development of the evocative picture surface. Once this had been arrived at paradigmatically, it could then be tried out for its capability to sustain meaning and yield a range of poetic expression.

Painted 1912

GOLGOTHA

Oil on canvas, 68½×75¼"
Museum of Modern Art, New York City. Lillie P. Bliss Bequest

Having explored the construction of the picture, the painter could feel free to develop the colored crystal of the surface in as rich and meaningful a way as possible. The translucent color and the hierarchic structure of the forms may have stirred up in him, during this work, memories of rural glass paintings and of the solemn Russian Byzantine icons which, as a young painter, he had seen and admired in St. Petersburg collections, although in those days without effect on his personal style. Now, however, his own painting had come to a stage where he could really absorb the message of the icons.

At this time a crucifixion scene came to hand from among his early drawings, in which he had taken up this age-old motif of the icons and elaborated upon it a little. He used this scene as the basis for *Golgotha*, keeping a similar figurative inventory and arrangement. For poetic enhancement and the transformation of the worldly scenery into a further dimension, he relied entirely on his newly discovered rhythms of form and color.

That Chagall chose to paint a crucifixion as his first great religious composition need not surprise us. He had always held the figure of Christ in great veneration, regarding Him as the perfect man, who out of love took upon Himself the most absurd and at the same time the most wondrous act—His own death—for the world's salvation. As such He reappears time and again throughout Chagall's work, particularly during the bitterest times of persecution of the Jews, when He was the representative figure of the exemplary capacity for suffering by the believer, who despite the deepest sorrow does not despair of the love of God.

There is no need to overemphasize the religious background. There was a need to express something visionary; the discovery of the drawing supplied the theme, and then Chagall left himself open to the wonderful suggestions which came in the course of painting. In a conversation with Franz Meyer, Chagall recalled a situation during the creation of the picture: "Strictly speaking, there was only a blue child in the air. The Cross was of less interest to me." What did interest him was the vision. That the appearing vision is of the greatest importance is shown by the central figure itself, which is not intended as the crucified at all, but as one resurrected into childhood, and at the same time as a messenger of salvation, descending from above.

The scenery is quite unreal. Circles and far-ranging arcs mark out an active cosmic field. The dark, complementary colors of red and green give the basic color harmony. Red is the color given to the earthly zone, into which it subsides as a dark brown-violet, and is reflected in the light-rose color of the distant islands, which glow with phantasmal light beyond the colored strip of water. Green is the color of the heavenly zone. Here, by means of a complex maneuver of dark segments, a great circle is made around the Christ figure. Through this circle shines a clear yellow, which also touches sea and boat with its light. A connection is created with the two attendant figures at the foot of the Cross by their position in the path of light streaming out from the transverse beam. The green of the heavenly zone flows down tenderly upon the small female figure standing to the right of the cross in a daintily embellished robe, with her left breast exposed as in the portrayals of the nursing Madonna in the old icons. Out of the red zone looms up the gigantic prophetic figure of a lamenting man, clad in a multicolored Oriental garment with gradations of iridescent color ascending to red-violet and finally interweaving with the green. The spiritual blue is assigned to the floating Christ Child, and the entire color sequence is culminated in its isolated light. In a darker hue the blue is reflected in the strange flamelike sail of the boat which is about to glide over the pale-blue band of water to the islands beyond. The boatman looks angrily across at an ugly gnome in Oriental garments as he drags away the ladder—one of the instruments of Christ's torture in the Byzantine iconography.

However strange this scenery may seem in relation to the conventional imagery of the crucifixion, within the magical dimension of the picture it achieves meaning and coherence. Within the crystalline structure of the evocative plane, everything depicted moves into another dimension, open to all the evocations of the miraculous, and takes on the tone of fable, fairy tale, and legend—the realm of appearance, where all wonders are possible. All the formal work that went into the construction of the picture was directed toward creating this "field of appearance."

In October 1912 the picture was exhibited at the Salon d'Automne, to which Chagall had been invited through pressure from Delaunay and Le Fauconnier. This was the official salon where Chagall made his debut. Although *Golgotha* hung in company with the pictures of Delaunay, Le Fauconnier, Gleizes, and the artists of the Section d'Or, it must have seemed very strange. In September 1913 Herwarth Walden exhibited it together with *To Russia, Asses, and Others* (colorplate 5) and *Dedicated to My Fiancée* (fig. 18) at the First German Autumn Salon in Berlin, and it is interesting to imagine how Franz Marc and Paul Klee would have stood musing before this picture, in which so many of the pictorial ideas stirring in their own minds had already been realized. Chagall's pictures met with an enthusiastic reception in this milieu, and the Berlin collector Bernard Koehler, patron of the Blaue Reiter, bought *Golgotha*.

Painted 1912

THE SOLDIER DRINKS
(Le soldat boit)

Oil on canvas, 43¼ × 37⅜″
The Solomon R. Guggenheim Museum, New York City

The Soldier Drinks is one of the first among the burlesque figure pictures describing a piece of reality remembered from the warmhearted atmosphere of small-town Russian life. It was preceded by a small gouache which already contained the individual details and basic layout of the composition, and which belonged to a series of gouaches recalling characteristic human types who had lent color to the environment of Chagall's youth: soldiers, the gendarme, tradesmen, carpenters, the barber, street musicians. His fantasies were now moving closer to that remembered life, whose fullness and warmth became represented by these types. Like the figures of classical comedy—such as we find in the commedia dell'arte or in the plays of Molière—they represent typical forms of human behavior, and like those characters they are stylized to fit their role, with humor and affectionate mockery.

The mythological scenery of Chagall's work retreats, and the human figure in its real-life aspect steps into the foreground. The far-ranging use of poetic metaphor which inspired the great paintings we have considered up to now is replaced by a closer, inquisitive, and often amused relationship to the reality of man as protagonist in the human comedy, with all the little details of his life's circumstances. The poet Chagall now descends from the esoteric regions of his dream world and comes to grips with reality, but by this time he has prepared his means of expression, so that even out of the more banal side of reality he is able to form his counterimages.

The soldier, in dress uniform and with his sword, the pride of his trade, is depicted half-length, sitting at a rough bar. With curled mustache and red face, he stares at the viewer. He is making a terrible fuss, stressing what an important person he is by a martial wave of his hand. He bangs on the table, demands a new glass, and gets so excited in the midst of all his boasting that his cap flies off. The samovar stands solidly on the broad table flooded with evening light streaming in through the window from the glowing sunset sky behind a peasant hut. We are even told what our hero is bragging about; the half-dancing, half-amorous little couple indicates that the tale is one of gallant adventures. This is how Chagall in his youth may have seen the village heroes and Casanovas at the village inn, gazing at them with both fear and astonishment.

The formal organization, robustly constructed of firm horizontals, verticals, and diagonals, also follows the trend toward realism. The previous rotating shapes and spirals which symbolically suggested the presence of cosmic, visionary, and legendary elements have been replaced by the plain and simple grid of verticals and horizontals, subject to the law of gravity, which fits with man's normal way of looking at life. Also the color is closer to reality, despite all its poetic heightening, and the volume has become fuller without disturbing the plane. A comparison with *The Poet* (colorplate 9), made only a few months earlier and showing a comparable constructive design, shows quite clearly the process of creating form and content with pictures distinctly remembered from reality.

The fact of living in Paris and having become familiar with its pulsating life, together with a new optimism generated by the success of his pictures, must have encouraged Chagall to make this advance toward reality. But this step led the way toward the next challenge, which was to prove crucial to Chagall's future development: discovering the point of miracle and legend in reality itself, and revealing this in painting.

Painted 1912–13

THE FIDDLER
(Le violoniste)

Oil on canvas, 74×62¼"
Stedelijk Museum, Amsterdam. On loan from the State
Collection

The Fiddler is the largest and the richest work in the series of figure pictures in which Chagall was bringing to life the typical characters he remembered from his childhood days. It was preceded by a small gouache dated 1912, one of a group of little pictures which came in an unending stream from Chagall's dreaming fantasy as he put his memories in order.

Certainly the fiddler had always been in Chagall's mind. Ever since 1908 he had constantly appeared in a variety of scenes. He was a central figure in the festivities of the Jewish community in the Russian suburb, and his tune accompanied the basic events of life—birth, marriage, and the funeral. By making his appearance at these important moments in life, he became an almost legendary figure—the attendant of human destiny—in the life pattern of the community. He appears as such in Chagall's pictures of births, weddings, and funerals. But to him the fiddler was also representative of the artist; a solitary individual, isolated by the strangeness and mystery of his art, he had communion with the powers of the beyond. Thus in *The Dead Man* (fig. 13) of 1908, Chagall has already expressed this idea in the symbol of the fiddler on the roof, a metaphorical figure who can be identified with its creator and becomes a kind of synonym for Chagall himself.

Although originally intended, like the drinking soldier (colorplate 11), as another typical figure from Chagall's remembered *comédie humaine*, *The Fiddler* has a strong legendary undertone. The lonely Jew with his fiddle looms up as an enormous figure before a snowy twilight landscape adorned with the scenery of a Russian village, and thumps out the rhythm with his boot on the roof of a tiny wooden hut. In great swinging arcs the landscape surrounds him like the circle of the earth. The half-circle of the first plane supports the fiddler, and he occupies it as if it were his sector of the world. A blossoming fairy-tale tree, filled with birds, serves as a poetic emblem.

Three brightly clad tiny beings, grouped together, gaze up in wonder at the mighty fiddler who, with hypnotic eyes in a green face—for Chagall green is the color of trance and hallucination—stares fixedly at the viewer. Behind this foreground scene, and separated from it by a zone of inky darkness in which a church and houses indicate the village, appears the rounded prospect of the wide, twilit snowfield. Not a soul is to be seen here, but human footprints sweeping in a circle from right to left mark out a kind of road of destiny in the empty field. Houses with warm lamplight shining in their windows fence off the field against the pitch-black sky. Above all this darkness, as if lured forth by the fiddler's tune, floats on a light-blue ground a golden child with a halo, by its gesture seemingly following and blessing the trail of destiny indicated by the steps across the field. This is a delicate playing with suggestions and metaphors which should not be taken too literally but which, within the context, indicates the rapture of the fiddler and endows this "typical figure"—which is what it set out to be, according to the gouache—with a legendary existence.

The formal buildup bears out and illustrates this particular meaning of *The Fiddler*, which is far more spiritual than *The Soldier Drinks*. The figure of the fiddler is strongly emphasized and every detail is realistically defined, but the ornamental makeup of the surface arrangement, based mainly on black and white, the subtle correlation of the planes which is brought out particularly in the upper part by the diamond pattern, and the flat expanses of the picture space have the effect of incorporating all realities into the poetical dimension of the picture.

Chagall himself considered the picture important. He exhibited it at the Salon des Indépendants in 1914, and a drawing of it was later printed in *Sturm*.

Painted 1914

JEW IN GREEN
(Le juif en vert)

Oil on cardboard, 38⅝ × 30¾″
Private collection, Geneva

In 1914 Chagall was back in his Vitebsk. "Vitebsk is a place apart; a town unlike any other, an unhappy town, a boring town," he writes in his autobiography, where there were "hump-backed and leanbodied citizens, green Jews, the aunts . . . ." During the latter years in Paris, his fantasy had been constantly occupied with the typical figures of suburban Vitebsk, and now he was confronting them in the flesh. In an impetuous urge to work he tried to lay hold of this real world. He portrayed everybody and everything: mother, father, himself, his sisters, uncles, aunts, all who were patient enough or who couldn't get away, the kitchen, the bakery, the living room, and people at their familiar household tasks. Together with his old friend and teacher, the painter Pen, he went out and sketched from life all the scenes in and around the town. He was preoccupied with creating the "documentary," as he liked to call it, and he lapped up this reality until he was full to the brim.

Strange guests—old beggars, peddlers with a sack over the shoulder, Jewish itinerant preachers—crossed the threshold of his father's devout and hospitable home. One day along came the "green Jew." He was the "preacher from Slousk," not a rabbi but one of those wandering Jews filled with holy inspira-tion, proclaiming the word of God, their lives full of extra-ordinary poetic radiance. There he sat, quiet and lost to the world, in front of the samovar in the living room. "I had the impression," Chagall recalls, "that the old man was green; perhaps a shadow from my heart fell upon him." So this is how he has painted him—as a meek old man slumped resignedly in his chair, with his green, inspired face illuminated by the gold of his beard. He seems to sit on a stone wall, as if it were a bench, on which are carved the holy texts in Hebrew script, the basis of his existence. Against the dark background plane, upon which the shape of the old man casts a wavering shadow, the green-golden face shines out like the countenance of the prophet Jeremiah, but the shabby Russian visored cap shows he belongs to the present age. The old man's jacket, colorless with age, also keeps him within the confines of reality. But look at the hands, one golden and one white, emerging from the crumpled sleeves! As they rest upon the man's knees,

touching each other, the golden hand makes a connection with the face, sunk in meditation, while the other one, marble white, with its scanning forefinger seems to interpret and repeat the words of the chiseled script. By the unrealistic coloring alone, this pair of hands evokes the aura of deep meditation and the interpretation of the holy word which fills the whole being of the devout Jew. Despite all descriptive realism, these remarkable symbolic details are intended to make reality trans-parent.

If we compare this picture with the hallucinated inventions of Chagall's early Parisian years, such as *The Holy Coachman* (colorplate 6), a closer approach to visible reality is indeed quite evident in the *Jew in Green*. But equally clear is the endeavor to bring out something of universal significance, to transform the fleeting moment of observation into something enduring. Indeed, a whole group of now celebrated paintings were made with this intent—such as *Jew in Black and White*, *Jew in Red* (figs. 20, 21), and *Jew in Bright Red*—which out of chance encounters with old beggars and wandering Jews conjure up the eternal figure of the migrant rabbis and Jewish miracle workers who saturated the life of the Eastern Jewish community with their beatific holiness. If we compare these pictures with the earliest versions of the rabbi theme, which began in 1912 in the course of Chagall's portrayal of remem-bered typical figures and which reached a peak in the famous picture of the snuff-taking rabbi, *The Pinch of Snuff*, we notice how, because of the immediate confrontation with real-ity, the power of poetic revelation is strengthened.

In a discussion with Jacques Lassaigne, which Lassaigne recalls in his book published in 1957, Chagall himself, with special reference to *Jew in Green*, has described the circum-stances of the painting very precisely: "I start from the initial shock of something actual and spiritual, from some definite thing, and then go on toward something more abstract . . . . This is what happened in the *Jew in Green*, whom I painted surrounded by Hebrew words and script characters (this is no symbolism, it is exactly how I saw it, this is the actual atmo-sphere in which I found him) . . . . I believe that in this way I arrive at the symbol, without being symbolistic or literary."

Painted 1917

THE BLUE HOUSE
(La maison bleue)

Oil on canvas, 26 × 38⅛″
Musée des Beaux-Arts, Liège

Chagall's beautiful holiday month in Zaolcha came to an end, and by September 1915 he was forced to go to live in Petrograd. In order to avoid military service he went to work there in an office of wartime economy, which was supervised by one of Bella's brothers. The time was not wasted. Back once more in the cultural center of Russia, he was able to participate in some important exhibitions in Petrograd and Moscow, and was pleased to notice that he was regarded by the youth of Russia as one of the great talents of the avant-garde. This new fame strengthened his self-confidence. Shortly before the October Revolution, while he was still living in the metropolitan milieu, he became acquainted with a circle of important intellectuals, among whom were political friends of Lenin and such poets as Mayakovsky, Esenin, and Pasternak. They made him feel he was standing in the midst of a whole phalanx of bold intellects bent on forming the future, and this added fresh zest to his personal work.

In the summer of 1917 he went home to Vitebsk for a two-month holiday. During that time he painted a series of highly significant landscapes, among them the famous *Cemetery Gate* (fig. 22) and *The Blue House*. He again confronted nature directly and tried by precise observation to achieve the clearest possible definition of the perceived impression. He often worked from nature, in which case his friend Pen screened him from curious onlookers, but the pictures were completed in the studio. These are highly accomplished paintings, far superior to the "documentary" sketches registering all his new impressions that he made when he first returned to Vitebsk, which were done to satisfy a certain hunger for the reality of his homeland. They have, moreover, on this new level the exclusive character of the *tableau manifeste*.

In the foreground of *The Blue House* is one of those Russian wooden houses made of rough-hewn logs, standing on the narrow bank of the river Dvina and shored up against the slope by a support wall of red bricks. The front door opens onto a track running past the house. To the rear there is a path going down to the river, with sloping meadowland on either side. In the background, high up on the farther embankment and reflected in the river, stand the middle-class stone houses in the heart of Vitebsk, topped by the many-towered baroque silhouette of the monastery which stands like an immense crown against the warm-gray sky.

Everything is strikingly accurate, with the outline almost a little too sharp—rather like the exactitude of the conventional *vedute*. Nevertheless, some of the houses are not quite vertical, and occasionally the perspective is a little off. There is a rhythmic band of rose-colored posts at the lower edge of the town area, and even the bare embankment is curiously faceted by a sequence of geometrical forms and undulating bands. The river takes up this prismatic ornamentation in a mirror reflection and carries it over to the opposite bank. All this creates a gently moving equilibrium not only of the individual groups of forms but also of the spatial arrangement of the planes, which, despite their apparent perspectival accuracy, always lead back in their faceting and interlacing to the surface. It is as though one were looking through a pane, and everything lying behind it had the appearance of being pressed into a flattened dimension.

The principal object to catch the eye is the log hut, and here the artistic manipulation has been carried out with consummate skill. When we look closely we see that this hut, so realistic in appearance, is composed of entirely abstract forms. What in reality would be the rafters have become a purely abstract pattern, making an astonishing contrast with the realistically treated chimneypot. The vertical junctions of logs at the corners of the hut become rhythmical rows of small circular forms, which at the right-hand corner of the hut multiply merrily to form a whole cluster of dangling circles. The horizontal layers of logs create a contrasting rhythmical motif, which in turn becomes disturbed by the crooked and quite unrealistically designed windows. The hut is also part of the surface pattern and plays a major part in the rhythmic to-and-fro movement of the planes which we have already noticed in the landscape on the left. What has happened here is the artistic transformation of the natural scene into the poetic vision, for which Chagall has used the same means he invented for himself in Paris in the course of his encounter with Cubism, but which he now has developed in direct contact with nature and then reapplied to the entire organization of the picture. The Cubist doctrines are now linked firmly with reality. They are being "developed and applied in contact with nature," as Cézanne had desired to do, but are already moving into the regions of free poetic expression.

The color too has its independent significance. The hut is colored in a radiant blue which sets the basic tone from which the color melody is developed. The picture appears in a radiant setting, as if it were inserted in a crystal of color.

Painted 1917–18

THE PROMENADE
(La promenade)

Oil on canvas, 66⅞ × 64⅜"
State Russian Museum, Leningrad

During the winter of 1917–18, soon after painting the Vitebsk landscapes, Chagall created three of his most famous figurative compositions: *Double Portrait with Wineglass* (fig. 24), *Over the Town*, and *The Promenade*. They too were painted in Vitebsk, and show that exuberant zest for living which went hand in hand with the new phase of artistic accomplishment he had achieved. To that must be added the political atmosphere—the exhilarating sense of freedom and optimism generated by the October Revolution, which had just taken place. For the Jews the revolution meant true liberation; at last they were entitled to the same full rights as every other citizen of the state. Humiliations such as the young Chagall had experienced during his studies in St. Petersburg, where Jews were allowed to stay only with a special residential permit, were now out of the question. And, as an artist, Chagall belonged to the avant-garde, which had everything to gain from these revolutionary changes. In addition, there was the happiness with Bella to put a golden glow on life despite the many adverse circumstances of the outside world.

So these large-scale pictures indicate a high-spirited, even exultant attitude to life, and they all center on Bella, against the background of the home town. In the *Double Portrait* the elated Chagall rides on the shoulders of the light-footed Bella, waving his wineglass. In *Over the Town* the enchanted pair floats gaily over the rooftops of Vitebsk. In *The Promenade* Bella in ecstatic jubilation flutters like a flag in the wind, held up in the sky on the arm of Chagall, who is laughing with joy and is dressed in his best clothes.

The pair has walked across the wide meadows in front of the town, a curving vista of little boxlike houses and the domed church. Above them stretches the broad light sky,

against which their figures are sharply outlined. They intend to have a picnic, and a bottle of wine stands ready on the flower-patterned cloth they have spread out. Then, all of a sudden, in the painter's exuberant fantasy Bella takes off like a bird from the ground and leaps like a ballerina at the end of his arm against the immense backdrop of the sky.

This ecstasy is in accord with the expansive decorative character of the picture. The dancing double figure extends over the plane like an ornamental emblem. The precious ornamentation of Bella's skirt pleats, as in a Futurist rendering of movement, greatly emphasizes the swinging effect of her floating figure. This ornamental stratification of form goes through the whole picture, arranging the meadow into a geometrical pattern, grouping the medley of cubic houses, reaching up into the sky in a variety of transparent geometrical forms, and culminating in the exuberantly patterned picnic cloth, which appears purely as a surface ornament. All Chagall's experiences gained from Cubism and Futurism—together with those from Matisse—have clearly gone into the making of the picture, but they are used to bring about a closer description of reality, even if the style is a little in the manner of poster art.

The precise drawing, the sharp contours, the clear and neat buildup of the cubic forms are all very striking, and so is the sonorous coloring, which remains within the bounds of realistically possible color tone. This lends the utterly fantastic scene a remarkable air of credibility. It is the same kind of meta-realism which had developed in Chagall's years in Vitebsk—a surrealistic moment in which the real and the fantastic merge into one, the sort of thing Apollinaire had in mind with his term *sur-naturel*.

Painted 1920

COMPOSITION WITH CIRCLES
AND GOAT
(Composition aux cercles et à la chèvre)

Oil on cardboard, 15 × 19½″
Collection the artist

This small sketch in oil on cardboard was painted in Moscow, where Chagall went to live in May 1920. Despite its unassuming appearance, it does acquaint us with a new field of activity for Chagall and with some new and somewhat surprising pictorial ideas. As flat as a poster design, it shows a simple balancing act made up of geometrical elements: two circles, of light and of dark blue, rest one above the other and are poised on a white beam which seems to be rocking on the fulcrum of a white square. A slanting, slightly curved green plane indicates a pendulum movement. Built into this seesaw game is the marionette-like figure of a young man in a violet visored cap, who seems to support himself on the balancing beam, and whose whip shows him to be a circus trainer. His own attributes are only a tiny bird and a cheerful goat with a little bell around its neck—a constantly recurring Chagallian emblem for animal joyousness.

Without a doubt this little scenic design had something to do with the stage or cabaret, for Chagall was very much involved with the theater at that time. In 1919 in Petrograd he had, on his own, worked on the sets for two of Gogol's plays, having been stimulated by various contacts with theatrical people. In 1920 in Moscow he was occupied with designs for Gogol's *The Inspector General*, which include many geometrical, Suprematist formal elements. In the end, none of these numerous and still existing designs was put into execution, however. Only once, in the Jewish Theater in Moscow, was Chagall able to become really active for the stage, doing the sets for three small plays by Sholem Aleichem. From then on, his enthusiasm for the theater never waned.

Despite the incidental character of the picture here it makes us aware of fundamental trends in Chagall's perception of the theater. It shows that he envisaged the theater as a thoroughly artificial counterworld, void of any naturalism, where the action is set in motion by forms and figures, and where variety turns and clowning also have a part. He looked on the actor in a similar way—as indicated by this painting—more as a figure and marionette than as the performer of an anecdotal or psychological role. Whoever writes the history of the modern theater ought not to overlook these early suggestions of Chagall's.

No less enlightening about his way of thinking at that time is the balancing of the elementary geometrical forms. These are doubtless of Suprematist origin, resulting from his association with Lissitzky and Malevich, especially in 1919, when he directed an art academy in Vitebsk and invited them to teach there. The conflict in their theories about art has already been discussed in the text, but the picture here plainly shows that the dispute over the abstract-constructivist aspirations of Suprematism was still occupying Chagall's mind. Although from the time he arrived in Paris he had fully recognized the significance of abstract elements in pictorial construction, and quite certainly must have discussed this problem with Delaunay, he used these elements only to reveal more fully a certain poetic vision. Now for the first time he examined these forms in terms of independent elementary structure, albeit within the sphere of the stage and its decorative-monumental possibilities. What may have encouraged him to do this is a feeling of uncertainty created by Malevich's theorizing and the wide effect it was having, together with a desire to reexamine his newfound meta-realism from an abstract viewpoint.

This interlude in style and attitude had no artistic consequences, but it did have personal ones. Chagall was becoming tired of revolutionary passion and the intolerant quarrels of the artists amidst the general misery. He longed to return to painting, and for him its Mecca was still Paris. Lunacharsky obtained the necessary passport for him, and in the summer of 1922 Chagall made his way first to Berlin and then in 1923 to Paris.

Painted 1925

THE WATERING TROUGH
(L'auge)

Oil on canvas, 57½ × 45¼"
Collection Vicomtesse Charles de Noailles, Paris

Much as the new French environment attracted Chagall, he never quite forgot his Russian world. Especially during the first years back in France the association remained very close. Indeed, the work on the hundred and more illustrations for Gogol's *Dead Souls*, filling the two years up to 1925, kept the scenes of the Russian country town very much alive in his imagination, as did the fact that Chagall had lost all his prewar pictures, left behind at the Sturm exhibition in Berlin and in his Paris studio, which impelled him during the first years after his return to Paris to paint a number of repetitions and variations of his important early works. Apart from direct replicas—the two renderings of the *Jew in Black and White* and *The Birthday*—it is not difficult to recognize the later versions, because of their more sensitive use of color.

In the course of this work, earlier gouaches with motifs of Russian rural folklore came to hand, which Chagall now made into large pictures. Thus *The Watering Trough*, which also exists in a later version and as a lithograph, goes back to a gouache of 1912. Apart from the little fairy-tale bird, which is a new addition here, the composition is quite accurately repeated. It shows a peasant woman bending forward in a very expressive pose, rearranging the feeding trough for a droll, distrustful-looking pig. The widespread branches of a tree overshadow the rural scene.

But the color is quite different and shows a remarkable change from the early gouache with its motley folkloristic and Expressionistic use of color. It is an example of the new "French" coloring, though raised to the slightly phantasmagorical elevation which is peculiar to Chagall. It is rich but gentle, based on a gently moving modulation of passages of sonorous, adjacent colors. Thus the whole ground of the picture which embraces the scene is a soft dark-blue passage, which begins with the exquisite ultramarine of the feathery, fabulous tree and, passing through the intermittent light of the violet, blends into a nocturnal Prussian blue mingled with slight accents of bluish green. The violet of the ground shows up again in the shaded parts of the peasant woman's garment, becomes stronger in the brown-violet of the trough, and weakens again in the delicate color accents of the fairy-tale bird. The green values culminate in the emerald body of the fabulous pig. The quite abstractly designed white form lights up the entire color sequence with a totally unnatural astral light which responds to the magical tone of the color instrumentation.

Taking account of the colors in this manner, one is surprised to notice that despite the sonorous tone the full range of the color circle has been touched upon: the red and green, the violet and the orange—a pure spot of color showing up on the flank of the swine, which, however unexpectedly from the objective viewpoint, is well-founded in terms of the color scheme. But the loud dialogue of the complementary contrasts has been toned down considerably, and moves into a softly and richly modulated harmony of color.

This new kind of sensitive coloring is something Chagall owes to his re-encounter with France. It had an effect on objective description, as we see, for example, in the abstract gold tone which flashes up without any objective justification on the green of the pig's flank. Similarly, the delightful little fairy-tale bird is not merely an additional item to enrich the objective contents of the picture; its delicate hues put the finishing touch on the color sequence. From now on it is a question to what extent Chagall's droll menagerie owes its pictorial life to narrative considerations or to the necessity of color development.

Painted 1925

PEASANT LIFE
(La vie paysanne)

Oil on canvas, 39⅜ × 31⅞″
Albright-Knox Art Gallery, Buffalo

Whenever possible, Chagall spent long months out of town, and it was only natural that on such occasions rural scenes such as in *The Watering Trough* (colorplate 17) came to mind. Chagall loved country life and was resolved, although without success at that time, to acquire a piece of land for himself somewhere. For him the nature, light, and landscape of France came as a new sensation, which he explored completely, with all his natural curiosity. Of course, he was still occupied with the etchings for Gogol's *Dead Souls*, which took him well into the fall of 1925, and these bound him in the spell of their Russian motifs. Thus, inevitably his Russian iconography often got mixed up in a very charming fashion with the new impressions of his French surroundings.

A delightful example of this synthesis is the cheerful picture of country life here. In the foreground a gay young country-man in the blue working jacket of the French peasantry, but with a Russian visored cap, is feeding his amiable little pony a sugar beet. Behind them is the curving panorama of landscape and sky, a great arc in which there is a variety of separate little scenes, regardless of the normal vertical position. To the left, following the extension of the diagonal of the horse's neck, is a red Russian log house. Portrayed in true Chagallian fashion, it allows one to see straight inside; there, beneath a hanging lamp, is a small group of men in animated discussion. To the right, along the rounded horizon, a gentleman and his coach-man drive off in an elegant chaise. A droll little peasant couple hops and dances in the open field. The whole merry scene might form a general background to the adventures of Gogol's arrant swindler Chichikov, and for all we know he might be the gentleman in the chaise. In fact, all the individual motifs of Russian folklore can be found again in the Gogol etchings.

But the light and the colorful atmosphere in which the objective details of the picture here seem to be bathed are far from Russian. It is the silken blue of the French sky that strikes the basic chord that resounds through the entire orchestration of color; it is the silvery light over the French landscape that casts its luster over the picture like an immaterial fluid. The rich variety of the colors is absorbed in this hazy gleam, and their volume of tone is reduced to a restrained harmony of richly differentiated hues. Chagall as a colorist has suddenly stepped into the tradition of great French landscape painting, which began with Corot and was introduced into twentieth-century painting by Renoir and Monet. Not that Chagall would have specifically had in mind this or that great master; first the astonishing encounter with the natural loveliness of France would have affected his sensitive eye almost unconsciously, and only later would he have perceived the logical connection with the French masters.

Here again the question arises as to what extent the objective motifs, seemingly scattered at random, are depicted for narrative reasons in this tale of country life or for the requirements of the color scheme. After all, it is quite remarkable that the lopsided house apparently gets its line of gravitation from the diagonal of the horse's neck, and its red as a contrapuntal response to the red cap of the young peasant; that the yellow of the horse's head is a prelude to the yellow of the roof; that from the pyramid of green formed by the horse's neck, mane, and beetroot leaves little sparks should fly off and fall into the upper blue zone, where they materialize in the green coach horse and the trousers of the peasant. Evidently the sensitive color scheme had a good deal to do with suggesting these little scattered scenes—but only to a certain extent, of course, because the synthesis of objective detail and color formation is indivisible. One spurs on the other, in a lively dialogue. That is the mark of the truly creative colorist.

Painted 1927

EQUESTRIENNE
(L'écuyère)

Gouache on paper, 20⅛ × 26″
Private collection, Switzerland

Midway through the work on the gouaches to La Fontaine's *Fables* Vollard proposed a new plan which filled Chagall with enthusiasm. He was to create illustrations on the theme of the circus, for which a suitable text would be found. Under these circumstances Chagall was entirely free as to choice and style of the individual scenes, and he made thorough use of this freedom. Whenever the opportunity arose, the two of them went to the Cirque d'Hiver and surrendered themselves to that artificial circus world which had been dear to Chagall since childhood. The fact that the enterprise failed in the end did not really worry them. Close to twenty large gouaches materialized in 1927, squeezed in between the illustration of the *Fables*. Chagall called them his *Cirque Vollard*, in memory of the unfinished plan.

They have hardly anything in common with the circus scenes he actually watched. They are purest *Cirque Chagall*—pictorial parallels to the world of the circus, which in his fantasy Chagall sends somersaulting into the absurd. Wholly fantastic in conception, they exalt the magic circus world, in which everything seems possible, to the sheerest artistic unreality. A gigantic pipe-smoking goat enters the arena, or a clown with an open umbrella trots past on a four-headed cowlike monster, or the Eiffel Tower balances itself, puffing a pipe, on the back of a Liberty horse (fig. 29). These absurd scenes push their way into the bucolic, Arcadian world of the *Fables* like antic satyrs.

The equestrienne here also belongs to the series of the *Cirque Vollard*. However, she does not ride at all. In the chaste pose of a recumbent Venus she lies nude and relaxed on her white horse as if on a bearskin, like the living imitation of an antique statue. There is no thought of parody; this is more like one of those "living images" by which the popular fantasy spontaneously calls to mind the figures of the ancient gods. The traditional gesture of chastity is also entirely in accordance with popular ideas. The hand covering the lap holds a bunch of flowers in a manner befitting only a circus star, and the arm upon which she rests her head holds a golden fan to indicate the ease with which her balancing act is performed.

Above the nude lady arches a sky of the loveliest lapis lazuli in which appear two moons, pale and golden, and thus the white of the horse and the female body are transformed into astral light, and the seemingly banal scene is removed into a mythical dimension, already suggested by the antique posture.

Gouache was an excellent medium for this kind of poetic enhancement of a subject and for the playful inventions of dreamy fantasy. The small size of paper meant that only slight hand movements were called for and that there was a freedom of improvisation without the demanding responsibility of a large picture. Moreover, the quality of the medium easily allowed corrections to be made. All these factors gave the artist great scope for playful fantasy.

Chagall's entire oeuvre has been borne along by the undercurrent of a ceaseless flow of pictorial ideas, which he literally discovers on his paper, in quiet hours or at nighttime, and he himself is often astonished by the world of forms taking shape before his eyes. These are not just chance happenings on the fringe of his great work, they are its very source; almost all his major paintings fall back on such spontaneous inventions. Also his series of black-and-white etchings—the *Fables* or the Bible illustrations—are based on a set of colored gouaches. Because of the flexible technique of gouache, an uninterrupted connection with the wellspring of imagery in the unconscious mind can be established. The gouache is the vehicle which brings the picture store, hidden in imagination and fantasy and blocked by everyday events, up to the surface and into view.

Painted 1929

FRUITS AND FLOWERS
(Fruits et fleurs)

Oil on canvas, 39⅜ × 31⅞″
Private collection, Paris

The encounter with the countryside of France, together with its intellectual and artistic influences, brought about a thorough change in Chagall's attitude toward color. The bold and vigorous palette, with perceptible undertones of Russian folklore, made way for more subtle coloring. This no longer stressed the dramatic contrasts brought about by the dialogue between pairs of complementary colors. Far more, it sought the crescendo and diminuendo of the lyrical color developments from a basic tone which can be effected by the modulations and gradations of neighboring colors in the color circle. The brighter color values form enlivening accents in the breathing modulation of the colored surface, which tends slightly toward the monochrome. This produces a flowing, floating light, not projected from any real light source—the sun or a lamp—but streaming forth from the light values of the actual skin of color. The result is a tender, dreamy, lyrical atmosphere for the expression of the theme and emotions of the picture. If we wish to find a comparison in the world of music, with which the painter himself would wholeheartedly agree, we must think of Mozart—who became Chagall's favorite composer.

In describing the chromatic changes which were taking place in Chagall's painting, I have already discussed in principle the coloring of the picture here, *Fruits and Flowers*, which is a classic example of the new and "French" coloring. As an art historian, I would like to particularize this "French" element—especially in regard to the dreamy picture before us. There is Cézanne, for one, whose thesis that the art of painting is founded not on "modeling" but on "modulating" evidently forms the basis of Chagall's picture. But there are also allusions of a different kind: the basket of fruit upon the violet cloth is like a salute to Bonnard; with the porcelain blue of the background, Renoir comes to mind; and the glimmer of the rich color web of the flower arrangement is a reminder of the later Monet, for whom the whole material world transformed itself into a glittering web of color.

Chagall did not quote these great French colorists directly, however—instead, there was a constantly renewed and complex dialogue during the act of painting, when Chagall was not too proud to recall a precept or example which would be helpful to him. Once in the Musée d'Art Moderne in Paris, when I happened to be hidden by a screen, I observed how Chagall studied a still life by Bonnard very attentively for a long time, then went across to a portrait by Vuillard, and afterwards returned to the Bonnard. Having discovered what he was seeking, he left the museum. It is these intimate dialogues with the masters who have aspired to something of the same kind and have achieved it which can give useful hints while the work is in hand and are included unconsciously and without any direct reference.

The color in the picture is a development of a sequence from violet (the table) through blue-green (the flower piece) to blue (the ground). The point was to produce a general tone with all the derivations from that tone. The general tone is blue, which cools down to blue-green and warms up to violet. The ring of red-violet roses, the powdery white of lilacs and lilies, and the concentration of livelier color accents in the fruit basket, which is a slightly intensified repetition of the entire color display—all these are colored paraphrases on the basic motif. It was a matter of raising up a floating, limpid blue, which has no material existence whatever and is only present floating immaterially in the harmony of the modulated colors. In the end, this radiance of blue comes to illuminate the entire picture. The material color has been transformed into immaterial color-light.

The meditative and evocative strength of the painting conjured up in Chagall's fantasy the tender little scene which dimly appears in the blue of the ground—the graceful figure of a girl, with two genii hastening to meet her. Behind the girl stands a startled fowl, and below there is a wooden fence—so the Russian provincial scene is given a token of recognition at least in one small corner. This playful figurative paraphrase is a sort of poetic embodiment of the tenderness the painter felt toward the simple beauty in the things he painted.

Painted 1931

EQUESTRIENNE
(L'écuyère)

Oil on canvas, 39⅜×31⅞"
Stedelijk Museum, Amsterdam

Compared with the previous grotesque circus scenes, the circus theme here is rendered in thoroughly classical style. The cautious handling of color to capture the delicacies of tone has also had an effect on the subject matter. Beauty, elegance, and a certain sweetness, all of which were looked upon with suspicion by the young Chagall during his early Parisian years, now became meaningful key words for him as his understanding of French tradition deepened. Similarly, he now came to recognize the word "decorative," of which a master such as Matisse was not in the least afraid, as something of positive value.

Chagall was living through a very happy period in those days. Theaters, concerts, and the mundane social life brought him into close contact with the fashionable society of Paris. He enjoyed this side of cosmopolitan life, which was something new to him, and as he was now a celebrated painter he could feel part of the artistic élite of this city which set the tone for the rest of the world. This too is reflected in the elegance of the picture here.

The graceful girlish figure of the circus horsewoman, who, with the soft pink of her embroidered dress and the red of her fan, sets the only higher color accents in the scene, poses calmly on the richly decorated saddlecloth of her white horse. It is a true fairy steed with the precious burden of a beautiful princess on its back, such as we may imagine from the *Arabian Nights.* With its gently bowed head it holds a garlanded violin. The rider herself is being embraced by her young lover, who is wearing a green velvet coat; thus the theme of the loving pair, which haunted Chagall's art throughout the years and even turned up in the flower pieces as if in a secret love nest, is touched on again in this extraordinary setting. The double figure on the broad back of the horse fills almost the entire picture plane. At the upper left near the edge of the picture, standing on some scaffolding which might also be a window frame, the small figure of a peasant fiddles a love tune; in the lower right in the moonlight is the scene of a village where a grotesque trio of man, cow, and cock make music for an exuberantly leaping clown. Both are poetic marginalia, as usual, which accompany the intimate mood of the two protagonists with a burlesque scherzo—as in *Midsummer Night's Dream* (colorplate 23).

Despite the distinctness of the contours, the paint has been applied in a very flaky manner. Its *sfumato* gives a floating quality. Here again, as in *Fruits and Flowers* (colorplate 20) of 1929 (indeed, the *Equestrienne* was preceded by a gouache of 1929), there is a tendency toward the monochrome, which, by way of the modulations of the blue, velvet-green, and light gray, hovers around a general ivory-colored tone. This grisaille-like coloring is raised to a higher pitch by the richly elaborate red of the horsewoman, a constant reminder of her beauty.

This picture and *The Acrobat* (fig. 30), which materialized during the same period, are the highlights of the sweet and lovely style with which Chagall celebrated his rapport with the life style of France and his artistic success in the society of Paris. But then times changed.

Painted 1938

WHITE CRUCIFIXION
(La crucifixion blanche)

Oil on canvas, 61×55″
The Art Institute of Chicago

The menacing political conditions which, in conjunction with the general economic depression, were looming over Europe and raising storm signals in Germany in 1933 brought the happy years to an end. Anxieties returned. The persecution of the Jews began. The first pogroms took place, and not in Germany alone; anti-Semitism also made itself felt in certain areas of France. In all of this the startled painter might well have recognized the signposts directing him back to his Judaism.

In the spring of 1931 he had visited the Holy Land with the Bible illustrations in mind. Strengthened in his faith and filled with memories of the land of his forefathers, he began work on the Bible and continued it throughout the following years. Then came news from Germany which was inconceivable to Chagall. Moreover, in the spring of 1935 he and Bella were in Poland for a short while and there too experienced outbreaks of hatred against the Jews which distressed him deeply.

These grave omens clearly influenced Chagall's painting. The seriousness of his outlook on life increasingly called for a change of themes. As early as 1933 he painted the picture *Solitude*, full of melancholy contemplation, showing a sorrowing, exiled Jew wrapped in his prayer shawl and holding the Torah. Large compositions, imbued with the pathos of grief and sorrow, made their appearance. *The Falling Angel* (colorplate 27) occupied the artist over a long period. In 1937 he painted the gigantic *Revolution* (fig. 31), which he later cut apart. Also in that year, when the synagogues were on fire in Germany, he began work on the third large composition, *White Crucifixion*.

This painting is to be understood as a direct response to the events of the times; in its naive narrative style, which assembles separate scenes of cruelty and suffering around the holy figure, it appears like a mighty ex-voto. In the center, beneath a white flow of light, is the huge portrayal of the crucified, not as the bringer of salvation but as the symbol of the martyred Jewish people. The Hebrew inscription, "Jesus

of Nazareth, King of the Jews," together with the loincloth cut from a Jewish prayer shawl, points to the Jewish origin of the crucified. Hence we find at the foot of the Cross the Jewish temple candelabrum in shining glory, and floating above the Cross lamenting figures from the Old Testament.

Around this zone of holiness, which occupies the center of the picture, are grouped the scenes of disaster. To the left a rabble of soldiers surges up and over a hill to storm a burning village of overturned houses. A big boat loaded with soldiers and screaming women drifts across the river. On the right-hand side a storm trooper has reached the synagogue and set fire to it; he is about to drag the Torah rolls from their shrine after having thrown the holy implements to the ground. In the foreground the Torah burns with the white smoke of incense, while a Jew in his caftan hurries toward it with a gesture of lamentation. To the left a shouting man, clutching a Torah roll to his chest with both arms, hurries away with a bewildered backward glance at the synagogue. In front of him a helpless old man walks into a void. At one time the cloth on his breast carried the words "I am a Jew," which Chagall later obliterated.

The composition—with the flow of light slanting across the center of the void in which hangs the figure of Christ, around whom explode scenes of turbulent activity in flame and smoke—might call to mind the Mannerists; the scene of lamentation in the heavenly zone is indeed reminiscent of El Greco, whose major works Chagall had seen during a visit to Spain in 1934. The ragged constellation of the bright color values, which do not arrange themselves easily within the strange monochromatic ivory light, also adds to the scattered character of the composition. Yet I tend to think it is the characteristic qualities of the votive picture which bring about these peculiarly naive features. The idea of beauty and elegance which had satisfied Chagall for a while did not stand up to world events; the ex-voto replaced the picture of classical beauty.

Painted 1939

MIDSUMMER NIGHT'S DREAM
(Songe d'une nuit d'été)

Oil on canvas, 46⅛×34⅞"
Musée de Peinture et de Sculpture, Grenoble

During the troubled years of the late 1930s Chagall also painted some serene pictures, of an astonishingly new and sumptuous coloring. The harder times became, the more tirelessly he applied himself to painting and for a while was able to forget the political oppression in his artistic activity. Whenever possible he stayed outside Paris, so that he and his work should not be disturbed by the wild rumors running through the city. During the summer of 1939 he stayed in the district of the Loire, in rural seclusion, and it was there that *Midsummer Night's Dream* was painted. During our study of some of the other pictures we have already occasionally been reminded of Shakespeare's comedy of the same name; Chagall was very fond of it and read it again and again. The play comes to mind when, in scenes of tender and elegiac mood—as ir the *Equestrienne* of 1931 (colorplate 21)—the burlesque enters as a sort of counterpoint. In the picture here the burlesque also defines the scene, but displays a noticeable restraint and a certain melancholy.

According to the title, we should label the pair as Titania and her donkey-headed lover Bottom. Yet the erotic and passionate element is so patently lacking here that one could not imagine Shakespeare's pair, absurdly entangled in magical mystifications, as having really been the model. In fact, this motif of the animal-headed creature embracing a bridelike being can be traced back to Chagall's first Parisian years. In the 1930s it came up in numerous gouaches as a regular feature of his iconography, but never before was the relationship between the two figures portrayed with such lyrical tenderness. Although the gorgeously colored tree growing on the left might be seen as belonging to Shakespeare's enchanted forest, the red angel flying toward the pair and seemingly bringing them together or the small musical clown in the background has nothing to do with Shakespeare's comedy. The picture constitutes an independent invention, and one gets the impression that Chagall added the title later as a poetic analogy. The

mood of tender earnestness and the deep feeling shown in the way the animal-headed being seeks to protect the calm bride and at the same time to draw protection from her lead away from Shakespeare and suggest the personal situation of the painter in those harsh and fearful times.

The figurative invention seems to have sprung from a new, free play with color. Never before had Chagall entrusted himself so entirely to it, nor had the solid structure of the composition been so firmly fixed in a bed of sumptuous color. During a journey through Italy in 1937 Chagall had made a penetrating study of Titian. The richly woven web of color in Titian's later pictures gave Chagall the idea of a deeply felt, broadly and spontaneously composed mode of painting, which he has at last displayed here. The sonorous, abstractly unfolding sequence of colors, radiating the same green-gold light which was also so precious to the later Titian, now sustains the picture. Not only is it deployed in independent tone groupings without regard to naturalistic probability—as in the blue of the earth zone, the blossoming splendor of the tree, or the bright red of the angel, all of which are held together by a golden-green accord—but it also conjures up the scene by means of its evocative strength. The brown of the animal-headed man's clothes, the white of the bride, the magnificent tree like a great bunch of flowers already existed in the layout of color before being specifically formed into the figures of the lovers or into the tree.

If we compare this painting with *White Crucifixion* (colorplate 22) we sense that the topical themes so movingly portrayed in the ex-voto have been left behind, and the pure poetry of color has moved into the foreground. With this picture a new chapter in Chagall's painting began, which developed during the years in America and led on to the style of his later years. At the time of his flight from France, *Midsummer Night's Dream* was in his luggage, as an exemplary reminder of the autonomous strength of color.

Painted 1942

SCENE DESIGN FOR THE FINALE
OF THE BALLET "ALEKO"

Gouache on paper, 15×22½″
Museum of Modern Art, New York City. Lillie P. Bliss Bequest

At first New York City fascinated Chagall immensely. He went drifting about in it with a feeling of awe, as if in some gigantic piece of antinature. He never learned to speak English, but conversed in Yiddish with the small Jewish shopkeepers and artisans of Manhattan. More often than not they must have talked about Russia and the war, because whenever he returned to his studio afterwards his mind was always full of the martyrdom of man, tragic scenes of war, and conflagrations.

It was just as well for him, therefore, that in the spring of 1942 a commission came his way which steered his fantasy in a completely different direction. Léonide Massine, the famous Russian choreographer, was at that time engaged in staging a performance by the New York Ballet Theater of the ballet *Aleko*—to the music of Tchaikovsky and after the poem *The Gypsies* by Pushkin—to be given in Mexico City. Massine commissioned Chagall to design the scenery and costumes. For months on end the two Russians together worked out the ballet down to the last detail, completely caught up in the elevated intellectual atmosphere of their homeland. At the beginning of August the company moved to Mexico City, where the performance was staged on September 10. It was here that Chagall painted the four gigantic backdrops and, together with Bella, supervised the production of the costumes. He had brought the sketches with him from New York.

The reproduction shows one of these, the sketch for the backdrop of the finale. Only in a metaphorical sense has it anything to do with the story of Pushkin's poem, which tells the tale of a young poet who, after becoming a member of a gypsy band, falls in love with the leader's daughter; betrayed by her, he kills her and her lover and is banished by her father. For the final stage setting, Chagall had in mind a kind of tragic apotheosis of the art of poetry. He painted a wide prospect showing a town view of Italianate character on a red ground, alongside which, curiously enough, extend the broad low Alpine houses of Savoy, as if the painter were recalling the landscapes of Europe which he had seen on his last visit. To the left, a cemetery on a hill rounds off the landscape. Above the burnt-red of the earth stretches the vast expanse of the heavens, blackened by storm clouds. A white horse with a two-wheeled cart, looking like a battle chariot of the Homeric Greeks, hurls itself through the stormy darkness; its faintly classical appearance stirs a memory of Pegasus, the winged horse of the muses. The bright shape surges up toward a warm golden circle, bearing the seven-branched candelabrum, which lights up the somber sky like a star of consolation. Thus the fate of young Aleko, of whom Pushkin wrote, called up a response in the fantasy of Chagall, not in any particular detail but only in its general sense—as a symbol of the poet's soul which, refined by suffering and death, comes at last to its deliverance. The color, in the threatening confrontation of red and black, fills the legendary background scene with pathos.

Already during Chagall's last year in France before the war, in the pictures he painted in Gordes, this pathos was becoming apparent in his color, which was sonorous in tone and broadly laid on, so that the large patches of color could exert an independent power of expression. This independence of color was strengthened during the American years and took on a serious and often tragic character because of the disastrous circumstances of the times. It was the most important pictorial means to sustain and reinforce the great poetic metaphorism which Chagall now introduced into his painting, and which was the real artistic event of the years of his American exile.

Painted 1943

THE JUGGLER
(Le jongleur)

Oil on canvas, 43½ × 31″
Collection Mrs. Gilbert W. Chapman, New York City

The Juggler is a major picture of the American war years. A very serious and mystical painting in the full sense of the word, it is filled with a personal mythology which avoids any literary symbolism. The signs are esoteric and ambiguous; they seem to suggest something real and then shift to the unreal, yet they are readable as an allegory of a personal confession.

The central figure dominating the picture is a circus ballerina with a leg flung up in the kind of acrobatic posture which first appeared in a picture of 1913 (now missing) by Chagall, showing three acrobats; the pose survived in his iconography as a hieroglyph for the circus theme. This representational figure has a cocklike bird's head which is masculine in features and expression; two blossom-white, angelic wings transport this strange hermaphrodite-demon into another world. Thus the figure is woman, man, animal, demon, and angel all at the same time, comprising all manifestations of humanity.

Having become aware of this, one quickly discovers significant references suggested by color. The dark cobalt blue of the dancer's tights, garnished here and there with signs of the moon, identifies the lower part of the figure as belonging to the female, or lunar, zone. Above the light green of the upper garment rises the gold of the cock's head and of the arm which clasps the upflung leg, suggesting without any symbolism but by the resonance of the color alone the masculine, or the solar, element which the cock frequently represents in Chagallian iconography. Above all this are spread the creature's white wings, which lift it toward the heavenly region. Thus the strange figure also incorporates the lunar, the solar, and the numinous—the three zones which enclose the manifestations of humanity mentioned earlier.

Over the outstretched right arm, like a limp rag, hangs an old-fashioned wall clock, Chagall's token for the passage of time. Thus the angel-demon stands for the timeless, the constant, and the eternal in humanity, which is within the reach of the artist above all other persons—though not of the artist as an individual, but of the id of the artist, which is clown, artist, man, woman, demon, and angel all together and belongs simultaneously to the lunar, solar, and numinous spheres. That this is not meant to be the ego of the artist is indicated by the fiddler, Chagall's representative figure for artistic man, who is small and subordinate here and produces his little tune, so to speak, in the bosom of the "super-id."

The figure is literally rooted in the dusky-warm ground of a circle, for roots and branches climb up the supporting leg. This circle at first glance seems to be a circus arena, and the small figure of a female stunt rider seems to justify this interpretation. But then the meaning changes: the rider is making her appearance on the roof of a Russian peasant house, and the imprint of one of its windows is on the leg of the standing figure. A red wooden fence, a small hut, and a tree appear to the left. The circus ring simultaneously becomes arena, village, and the earth—that is, a representational sign for the globe. In the upper part it seems nothing but an arena, with spectators seated around it, but lower down, embraced by an infinite blue, it assumes an unreal, cosmic character and can be compared to the sign medieval painters used to indicate the circle of the earth. Indeed, at the right, out of the infinite space surrounding it, emerges a rainbow. But this too turns unexpectedly into a kind of heavenly circus gallery, from which a large hybrid creature made up of woman and horse looks down into the earthly arena, while a trapeze artist at the tip of the rainbow, dressed like a bride, acknowledges the applause.

Through these intricate, mystical interrelationships the painting seems to enter the purest Cabalistic sphere. Yet the meaning is perfectly plain. The figure that appears as an animal-headed Egyptian deity is an interpretation of the artist, not of his ego but of the id which stands behind all individual expressions of creative art, the personified genius itself. Rooted in the earth, which is his playground, surrounded by the cosmos and reaching into it, absorbing all manifestations of humanity and growing through the categories of the lunar, the solar, and the numinous, and confronting fleeting time with durable pictures—it is in this form that the artist enters the arena and appears before the onlookers. There can be no more comprehensive image of the artist than that illustrated in the sublime pictorial metaphor of this picture.

Chagall arrived at this pictorial metaphorism, which he had constantly been aiming at in his work, during his years in America. At that time he was living a secluded existence in the state of New York, often being absent from the city for months. This detachment was very good for contemplation. He often thought of Russia and felt it was significant that he had set foot on American soil at the time that Russia was invaded. This bond with the fate of his homeland determined the earnestness of his artistic performance. He painted many crucifixion scenes and many pictures showing conflagrations and the ravages of the war. But among them we find such timeless pictures of destiny as *The Juggler*. In the mysterious, dark splendor of its color, in the esoteric character of its emblems, it is the paradigm of a pictorial metaphor which can transform poetic feelings and impulses into a pure image—into picture, emblem, and colored tone—beyond any literary and symbolic allusions. From this time on the work of the painter-poet Chagall was devoted to the development of this use of metaphor.

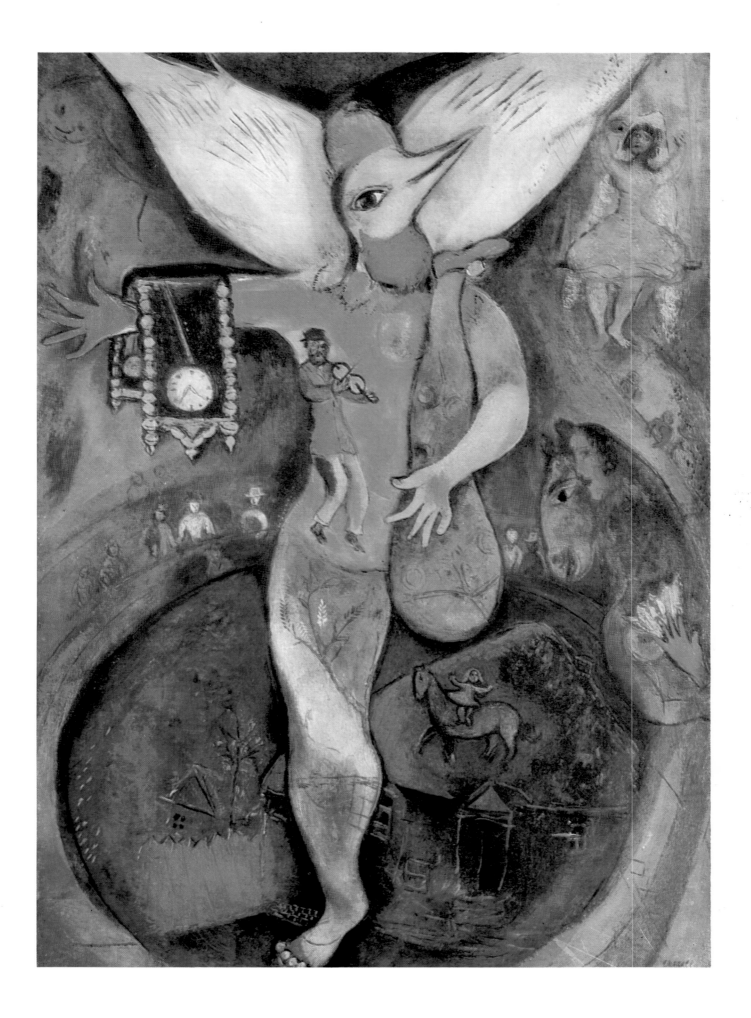

Painted 1945

THE WEDDING CANDLES
(Les lumières du mariage)

Oil on canvas, 48⅛ × 47¼"
Private collection

On September 2, 1944, Bella died at Cranberry Lake in the north of New York State of a virus infection which at first had not seemed at all serious. She had been the intimate companion of Chagall's life and work since his youth. Her death came unexpectedly, although on reflection Chagall felt he had recognized early signs of a quiet detachment, and Bella herself, as if urged by some dark foreboding, had concluded her literary work and put it in order with unusual haste. In 1935 she had set herself the task of recording the memories of her youth in her home town of Vitebsk and of her first encounter with Chagall. She had written them down in Yiddish, the language of her childhood. Both the books she left behind—*Burning Lights* and *First Encounter*—are radiant with the glow of memory of Jewish feast days in the cosy family circle and of the Eastern Jewish faith which imbued the reality of childhood with holy legends.

Bella's death was the heaviest blow Chagall could have suffered. It happened just when news was coming through of the liberation of Paris, which had stirred hopes in both their hearts of being able to return home soon. Hope and consolation now collapsed. Painting was out of the question for the time being. Bella's last words had been about her "notebooks," so in the months following her death, Chagall assisted their daughter Ida with the French translation of *Burning Lights* and wrote a preface lamenting "Basinka, Bellotschka from the mountain of Vitebsk, who is reflected in the Dvina together with the clouds and the trees and the houses."

It was not until the spring of 1945 that Chagall returned to painting. In his studio he came across a large picture, 98 inches wide, which he had painted in 1933. Entitled *The Harlequins*, it showed Bella as a half-length figure wearing festive clothes, in the midst of a variety of circus folk. A vaulting acrobat was presenting her with a transparent globe showing a picture of Vitebsk, while to the right a wedding procession made its way into the circus world. This picture Chagall now cut through the middle. From the left half he made the poignant painting *Around Her* (now in the Musée National d'Art Moderne, Paris), in which the magical globe with the vision of Vitebsk occupies the center, with a weeping, mournful figure of Bella by its side. The right half became *The Wedding Candles*, the title referring to Bella's book and its elevated mood.

Only the winged, goat-headed figure and the bridal pair have been taken over from the original picture. All the rest, above all the color and the mood, has undergone a complete change. The picture became one of twilight and nightfall. In a strangely overcast, dusky, hazy atmosphere, the bridal pro-

cession moves out of the Russian village, in front of the setting sun. An immense chandelier with burning candles hangs above the bridal canopy and carves in the nocturnal blue an aureole of greenish, ghostly light. It is in keeping with the dim color haze from which the bride emerges with her entourage, and it lights up a bare place across which straggle some village musicians with startled faces, playing their instruments separately. To the left the zone of nocturnal blue opens up. While the lone musicians move off toward the lower right, the small white figure of the bride proceeds toward the zone of midnight blue, into which she is led by a pair of lovers reclining on a cock's back; there the winged creature with the goat's head is waiting, the welcoming drink of night in its hand. Above, a celestial horn player descends from the blue, his gesture seeming to drive off the earthly musicians and at the same time to show the white bride her way.

Compositionally, the picture tends to fall apart because of these divergent directions. The color-light alone, with the half-circle of dark blue and the echo of the orange, holds the construction together with difficulty. It is the metaphor in the picture, the focus of all its elements of color, form, and contents, which ultimately creates pictorial unity. The little white figure of the bride is crowned by the whiteness of the burning lights above her, and is led on into the dark by the whiteness on the wings of the goat-headed creature. It is she who, herself like a light, guards the center of the picture and by her presence holds together the centrifugal elements. She is also the center of the metaphorical meaning which the painter was trying to discover and express. It is the picture of the Jewish bride, detached from all anecdotal and worldly associations, which finally emerges as the visual metaphor. As such Bella had entered his life, and as such he perceived the expression of her personality in her poetic works—"her style is the style of a Jewish bride in Jewish literature," he wrote in his epilogue. As such, too, she remained in his memory, reappearing in this form countless times in his later pictures. When toward the end of the 1950s he thought of decorating the little Calvary chapel in Vence with his religious paintings, the sacristy was meant to be adorned with his pictures to the *Song of Solomon* in memory of Bella, where she appears entirely in the mythical image of the Jewish bride.

This picture responds to a particular moment in life and interprets its poetic reality. Although it by no means belongs to Chagall's most outstanding works, it nevertheless reveals with extraordinary clarity the manner in which the painter reacted to the real events in his life and made of them a picture as a responding *imago*.

Painted 1923–33–47

THE FALLING ANGEL
(La chute de l'ange)

Oil on canvas, 58¼×65⅜"
Private collection, Basel

In his last American years Chagall frequently occupied himself with earlier pictures, and with the help of deepened life experiences and new artistic insight was able to bring them to completion. At the time he was living in High Falls, not far from New York City, in a small wooden house in an isolated valley. Seclusion and tranquillity were an aid to contemplation. Moreover, the hope and desire of being able to return soon to Paris—which he had already revisited for three eventful months in the spring of 1946—may have inclined him to bring things to a conclusion, in order to be ready for a fresh start.

In this state of patient meditation and expectation, one of the most important pictures of Chagall's oeuvre was at last completed: this was *The Falling Angel*. Twenty-four years had gone into the making of this significant painting. The individual phases of the picture mark decisive events in Chagall's life, which was frequently disturbed by the political happenings which toppled the old order in Europe and oppressed the Jewish people. By no means a political picture, in its imagery *The Falling Angel* encompasses all the anxiety and suffering of the times, continually punctuated by new disasters. In response to these calamities, this strange apocalypse, which had evolved from his personal mythology, formed in the painter's mind. Individual symbolic figures in it are given the task of representing the psychic complexes of fear, the desire for mercy, and protest—as was the case in Picasso's *Guernica*.

The first version—one could say the first prophetic warning to be inscribed on the canvas like the writing on the wall—materialized in 1923. It showed, as indicated by a small watercolor made a little later, only the figure of the falling angel, from whom a fleeing Jew is trying to preserve the Torah roll. In the early summer of 1922 Chagall had left Russia in the feverish aftermath of revolution and had returned to Paris via Berlin on September 1, 1923. At first he painted a series of repetitions and new versions of his earlier pictures, but midway through this work the new motif of the angel's fall presented itself, as an image of his personal flight before the angel of the revolution—angel or Lucifer, on that he did not commit himself. The Torah alone—which was also his art—had to be saved from subversion and atheistic outrage.

In 1933, the year when the pogroms of the Jews commenced and the coming war began to cast its shadows, Chagall confronted the picture once more, and the cast of characters was expanded. The solitary figure of the fleeing Jew as the representative of individual destiny now received as a background the town of Vitebsk, which for Chagall had always stood for his homeland and its people. The falling angel now bore along with it into the abyss a terrified and completely innocent traveler. The clock, emblem of the rhythm of historical time, followed this fall. The composition still remained unsettled and scattered, however, and again Chagall abandoned it.

At last in 1947—after war, flight, exile, and the destruction of the world from which the picture had sprung—it was brought to a successful conclusion. The surface was compactly built up, solid as a grim wall of thunderclouds. Fragmented and faceted like a crystal, interspersed with whitish portions, and marked with sharp outlines, this hard surface has taken the place of the previous perspective, still illusionist in conception, and has become the field. A somber light from the dark blue and the fragmentary white illumines this visionary field of the beyond. Like a firebrand the angel plummets through this gloom, with its wings spread out wide and one jagged wing tip hitting the sleeping village like a lightning flash. The helplessly extended arm and the one terrified eye which stares out fixedly from the center of the picture at the viewer signify that the angel, hurled into the picture by a supernatural wrath, is suffering the same fate that, in its fall, it inflicts upon the world. History's steadily ticking timepiece accompanies the fall, and the ordinary man, a clumsy and unsuspecting wanderer through this world, is sent crashing through an angular cleft into the abyss. In the face of such destruction, the terrified rabbi in his solemn violet garment snatches up the word of God and carries it out of the zone of apocalyptic fury.

Is there a gleam of consolation anywhere? In the midst of this tumult, between the terrified faces of the rabbi and the angel, floats a comforting star of golden brilliance, and from below, in the same golden tone, rises the head of an innocent creature, gazing astonished and uncomprehending at the calamitous scene, while a little blue violin plays a perpetual tune by itself. The comforting star is related to the golden circle of the clock pendulum and the aureole of the burning candle on the right. As small and sparkling fixed points, these signs of light impose a calm constellation over the surface, and in the wild nocturnal riot of the heavens design a kind of star picture of calm and consolation.

In the circle of light from the candle, two small and quite new figures appear: to the right is the crucified, wearing a Jewish prayer shawl for a loincloth; to the left, emerging from the garment of the falling angel, a mother and her child. The

smallness of the figures and their independence in the composition detach the little scene from the grand drama of events and make it a picture within a picture. As still as an icon, appearing in the light above the nocturnal village and pushed into the corner as if into a sacred niche in the dark vault of heaven, the consoling scene shines out at us, like a naive saintly image. As we thoughtfully read this picture, it slowly becomes clear what it seeks to illustrate: it is a pictorial parable on the impact of the wrath of God, who nevertheless is still a loving God. Clearly one cannot solve the various figurative and formal elements as one does a picture puzzle. The readability and unity of the picture are fulfilled in its poetic metaphor, in which the nightmarish events and cataclysms of our historical period are translated into vivid images and signs.

The striking impact of the picture and its capacity to support the visionary element rely to a great extent on the delib-erate use of the independent evocative power of color. After Bella's death, Chagall had thrown himself into work on the decorations for Stravinsky's *Firebird*, for which he had been commissioned by the New York Ballet Theater (fig. 40). During the work on those vast surfaces, color had come into full bloom all on its own; the setting was almost abstract in character. Then, in 1947, Chagall had done a series of goua-ches for the *Arabian Nights* which were meant to serve as designs for subsequent lithographs, and here too, inspired by the Oriental theme, he had surrendered to the splendor of independently used color. This renewed and deepened expe-rience of the independent power of expression in color and of the expanded application of it in large areas now had its effect upon *The Falling Angel* and led on to monumentality of color and form.

Painted 1947

FLAYED OX
(Le bœuf écorché)

Oil on canvas, 39¾×31⅞″
Private collection, Paris

The same monumental and allegorical power that we observed in *The Falling Angel* (colorplate 27) is displayed in *Flayed Ox*, which was painted at roughly the same time. This painting too goes back to an earlier motif, which Chagall had begun to work on in 1929, in remembrance of Rembrandt and also most probably of Soutine, who was his studio neighbor in La Ruche during the first Parisian years. But whereas in the first painting of 1929 the animal's body was arranged beside a bouquet of flowers and in front of a bright, wide landscape—in an impasto style with attention to color values, so that the painterly and still-life elements were predominant—in *Flayed Ox* it is once again the metaphoric quality and the color which elicit from the stark motif a parable of fate. Since the days of his childhood, when, during drives with his uncle Neuch the cattle dealer or in his grandfather's slaughterhouse, he had seen animals killed in the Jewish fashion, the slaughter of the animal had held an uncanny fascination for him, like the ritual of a sacrifice which had a deeply hidden meaning and for which a means of expression would eventually have to be found. His first studio in La Ruche was close to the slaughterhouses of Paris, and he recalls, "Dawn is breaking. Somewhere not far away they start cutting the throats of the cattle, cows bellow, and I paint them."

The hidden meaning which he wanted to paint now emerges as a picture and as a parable of the times. The gigantic, crucified body of the animal hangs before a nocturnal scene. In the skinned, raw flesh is still the agony of wanting to live, shown by the greedy lapping of its own blood. At the left a terrified cock rushes away. The drama takes place in front of a Russian village on a clear, bright, winter's night; against the background of huts piled up like boxes in the cold light of the snow, the lonely flayed colossus appears, like a sacramental offering, as a bloody banner and apotropaic vision of terror which contrasts to the peace of the place. The head of a peasant woman gazes compassionately at it across the roof of a house. The limp wing of an exhausted clock dangles out of a front window, as if time were ready to die. The sky is dark and hard like hammered metal. The surface is solid as a wall, as in *The Falling Angel*, and in the compact layers of its structure has lost all illusionist character. At the top right occurs a most unrealistic event which shifts the entire ensemble of figures and things, seemingly halfway realistic, to a visionary realm. Into the picture flies a bearded Jew, with outstretched arms, as a messenger of terror. As his bloody knife indicates, he is the slaughterer who has performed the sacrificial ritual. But he is also the terrified prophet who proclaims the terrible truth that only in the bloody sacrifice of the innocent does man come to recognize reconciliation and peace. Above him the burning candle, the Chagallian emblem for peace, warmth, and domestic tranquillity, threatens to go out. Now we can see more clearly that the picture is concerned with a new metaphoric interpretation of the crucifixion theme. The image of the crucified creature becomes a representative, universal sign for the message of the crucified Christ, detached from the narrower religious associations. During the war years, from 1940 on, Chagall painted many pictures with scenes of devastation—villages on fire, people fleeing—some of which depicted the crucified amidst human misery. None of these, however, has the rapt solemnity and timeless symbolism which we find here. The whole agony of the times has been gathered into one intense, definitive, and portentous metaphoric picture.

Already in *The Falling Angel* each individual figure and object was precisely defined and delineated; in the picture here, dark contour lines emphasize the forms of the objects. This produces a monumental effect and at the same time strengthens the intensity of the color. Like the dark lead strips in a church window, the black contours isolate the individual color areas, bring out their independent luminosity, and help to adorn the surface with a pattern of colored light. By means of this grand ornamental style, the objects are fixed in a crystalline, well-balanced, and solid grid, which, through the orchestration of color in individual, independent adjacent tones, glow with an unreal and enchanted light. If one looks into the magic prism of the picture plane, every realistic object becomes transformed into a pictorial sign and steps out of its materialistic confines into a further dimension. Object and symbol become one in the colored forms.

These allegorical pictures of destiny not only give final expression to the experiences and horrors of an entire period of life, but bring the coloring which began with the early crystalline, faceted "Orphist" pictures full circle. A new exploration into color now becomes possible. Chagall's exile is also at an end artistically; he leaves America, and in Paris begins a new period of work.

Painted 1954–62

THE FARMYARD
(La ferme)

Oil on canvas, 23⅝ × 28¾"
Private collection

In general, forms become more massive in Chagall's later pictures, which is in accord with the expansion of color into larger areas. One can even assume that it was just this effort to achieve a more intensive coloristic use of the picture plane—an effort which was considerably increased in Vence—which called for large solid forms to support the development of color. And in response to this, as a countermove, there is a more compact, ornamental, and lively treatment of the surface design, which is spread like a richly embellished carpet around the large areas of color. If in Chagall's earlier burlesque scenes the medley of fabulous beasts and bizarre performers went tumbling head over heels and filled the entire surface, inducing the color itself to vault and dance, now we find that the merry uproar and roguish humor which characterize Chagall's sense of humanity so charmingly are becoming calmer, more tender, and wiser.

The burlesque theme! It moves in colorful and festive procession throughout Chagall's entire oeuvre, and makes us smile when we think of his picture world, but it has also caused insensitive critics to put this great painter-poet into a corner with fairy-tale tellers. Chagall's humor and delight in the burlesque is never crude, offensive, or caricaturizing. He is full of tenderness and affection toward the funny side of nature and living creatures; he exaggerates and fondly puts the finishing touches on their amusing antics, playfully moving in those spiritual heights which are the home of *A Midsummer Night's Dream* or *The Magic Flute*. Like Paul Klee, he is delighted when occasionally humor overcomes grief.

For Chagall, the burlesque theme was linked from early days with the rural idyll. In the backyards of Vitebsk he had opportunity to understand the good-natured grumbling of the cows, the bleating of the goats, and the cock-a-doodle-doo of the roosters as a merry song of praise to the existence of creatures in harmony with nature. Ever since then, the apotheosis of the simple rural existence has been a recurring theme in his dream of life.

In addition, for Chagall the animal—and in this he is comparable to Franz Marc—is the creature which has always, uninterruptedly, been part of the great circle of nature which man has abandoned through willfulness, contradiction, and passion, falling victim to sin and grief. For Chagall the animal represents harmony and contentment with the cyclic destiny of nature; the innocent acceptance of being a part of nature's great ensemble of living things; and lastly, to quote a high-flown but perfectly justified phrase of Raïssa Maritain, "the peace of the universe," to which the restlessness of man, the cosmic troublemaker, stands in such evil contrast.

One such rural idyll is shown in the picture here. A large yellow cow, the countryman's friend and provider, marches eagerly across a meadow behind a Russian farmstead toward her feeding place, while a robust peasant woman carries up the fodder. A superb specimen of a pert rooster edges forward so as not to miss its pickings. A little tree, all blossom and tinsel and surely cultivated in some seraphic nursery, tries to steal the show from the fabulous cow, but like some droll heraldic sign the head of the cow and its cheeky competitor, the cock, remain stubbornly in the foreground, and their voracity makes us smile. This scene is wonderfully well observed, and, in the droll way it points out what nature can offer us, is full of the tenderest humor.

But let us beware of losing ourselves in anecdotal detail, because everything that this scene shows reaches us as a picture—that is, as a collected *imago* of perception of reality—through the magic prism of color alone. The great expanse of yellow stretches over the picture like a warm light and calls up the dreamy blue of the ground, and the dainty arabesques on rooster and tinsel tree refract the strong ground tone in tender gradations through violet to the delightful accent of the red in the cock's comb and to the green of the tree; the whole web of color is interspersed with fine passages such as these. In order to give a tranquil counterpoise to the dominant yellow, a fine ornamental pattern stretches across the whole surface, adding a special richness. Every poetic element in the picture arrives at its visual appearance only by this means, since it is indissolubly united to the form. That is the miracle of painting—making the wondrous more distinct and credible as a possible reality than plain visibility is able to do.

Painted 1957

CLOWNS AT NIGHT
(Les saltimbanques dans la nuit)

Oil on canvas, 37⅜ × 37⅜"
Private collection

Opposed to the burlesque is the tragic. Franz Meyer records that Chagall, referring especially to *Clowns at Night*, has noted that painting is "a tragic language." In a foreword to Fernand Mourlot's catalogue *Chagall Lithographs* of 1960, the painter enumerates the themes and ideas that colors have suggested to him during his artistic life, and pensively concludes the list: "... and, with old age, the tragedy of life within us and around us."

The elegiac mood permeated the years in Vence as a melancholy and slowly intensifying undertone, and increasingly produced pictures of a somber coloring. Chagall had always been fond of the nocturne, with the colors tuned to a minor key, and now it became the favorite motif; distinct from dramatics and despair, the mood is one of gay sadness. The emblem it carries on its banner, as Paul Klee once wrote in his diary, is "the merrily hopping tear."

The picture here shows circus folk and *artistes*. Discharged from the transient brightness of the arena, fallen from the dazzling instant of artistic achievement back into obscurity, the procession of illusionists wanders across the dark field under a stormy sky. A bleak hut squats under two sinister moons. The leader of the procession, a pale young violinist with lost eyes and a face like a tragic mask, looks across at us; he stares at us steadily, bending his ear toward his girl companion, who accompanies his violin tune with the darker tone of the flute. A bird-headed figure in clown costume, hardly distinguishable in the darkness, carries along a girl singing at the top of her voice. Her white face suggests she belongs to the spectral world of the violinist, to whose tune she is singing. A small group of singing and playing girls provides the chorus. One of them carries a faintly gleaming spray of blossoms, which, according to her glance, is meant for the pale violinist. So the forlorn troupe plays on through the sad, phosphorescent, moonstruck night, and only in its own music finds a spot of warmth.

Without question, the picture is of psycho-biographical importance. Chagall has always looked upon the life of the *artiste* as the image of his own humanity and of his personal "impossible task," as he likes to call it. He has always felt a deep brotherly affection for the figure of the tragic clown stumbling through life's mysteries and shadows—represented for him for many years by the actor Charlie Chaplin. More than anyone else, Chagall knows about the dark hours of the *artiste*, and in allusion to these the metaphor of the *Clowns at Night* came into being.

The blackish-blue ground is almost monochrome, with only a few muted color accents to enliven the undefined zone of darkness. The color looks as if it were sintered, encrusted, and sunken into the granulated structure of the ground, so that it is not so much the individual pigments but the whole crust of the color skin, that is, the material itself, which is illuminated. As a result, the black and the white also gain independent color strength as darkness and light. Chagall did not forget this coloristic experience; it shows up again in *The Big Circus* of 1968 (colorplate 36).

The nocturnal mood is not confined to this picture alone, although here it perhaps reaches the strongest pathos of expression. It also penetrates Chagall's biblical pictures and finds a special lyrical fulfillment in the four pictures to the *Song of Solomon* (see fig. 41) which Chagall dedicated to Bella's memory and which he had hoped to keep in the Calvary chapel in Vence.

Painted 1950–52

MOSES RECEIVING THE TABLETS OF THE LAW
(Moïse recevant les tables de la Loi)

Oil on canvas, 76⅜ × 51⅛″
Private collection, Paris

In Vence the biblical theme in Chagall's painting reached its peak. As the individual great biblical pictures materialized one after another—beginning with *King David* of 1951 and *Moses Receiving the Tablets of the Law*, and continuing in 1955 with *Moses Breaking the Tablets of the Law* and *The Crossing of the Red Sea*—and grew year after year into an entire picture cycle, the idea of a Biblical Message ripened in Chagall's mind; it is a plan which has continued to occupy him constantly. For this purpose he required an ecumenical public building free of all denominational bonds—not a museum or place of organized worship—where modern man in his restlessness could turn aside and contemplate the ancient religious legends of our origin, take away with him a glimmer of the message they convey, and later perhaps also discover their truth in his own life, as the painter himself had done. Originally he had had the little rural Calvary chapel of Vence in mind as a place for his pictures. When this plan came to nothing, he gave the main works of the painting cycle to the city of Nice, which has built a museum to house them.

It was no coincidence that the biblical theme made itself so strongly felt in Vence. As already mentioned in the text, it had entered Chagall's world of ideas in 1930, when Vollard commissioned illustrations to the Bible; until then, there had been no pronounced religious trend in Chagall's art. By the time of Vollard's death at the beginning of World War II, sixty-six etchings had been completed and a further thirty-nine had been begun. The war and the chaos that followed interrupted the work, and not until 1952, in Vence, was Chagall able to resume the gigantic task. It was concluded in 1956, and published a year later by Tériade (see figs. 59–63).

In conjunction with this work on the cycle of biblical etchings, the biblical theme also appeared in his painting and became a regular motif. Soon it also moved into the monumental field: in 1959–60 Chagall made the first window for the cathedral in Metz, in 1960–61 the windows for the Jerusalem synagogue, in 1964 the great tapestries—*The Creation, Exodus,* and *Entry into Jerusalem*—for the Parliament of Israel. The Bible also provided subject matter for ceramics, with which Chagall was at first intensely occupied in Vence, and for sculpture as well.

Clearly, the subject was completely in harmony with Chagall's inner world; he had needed only the impetus of a commission to perceive the Bible as a fulfilling theme for his art. Until then, on the occasions when he had used a religious subject, it had almost always been the theme of Christ, particularly the image of the crucified, which appeared in his work, and continues to do so, as a representative figure for the

sufferings of the world, even in scenes from the Old Testament. But now all the artist's ideas and imagery came bursting out in the form of a wholly personal iconography independent of all the scenes to be found in the history of art. The Oriental biblical scene became peopled with caftan-wearing Jews of the Russian ghetto, whom he had seen in real life, though the background scenery and the light came from the Holy Land itself, which had touched him deeply when he first saw it with Bella in the spring of 1931, and which he revisited with Vava in 1951, 1957, and 1962.

At the beginning of this monumental cycle stand the two archetypal figures of Jewish history, Moses and King David. The image of Moses, who received the divine Law and rose to be the ethical and political leader of his people, occupied Chagall for years; his biblical etchings include a whole series devoted to Moses. In painting, the picture here, together with the two painted in 1955, forms a Moses triptych. In the etching which corresponds to this picture, the lonely figure of Moses is shown before the dark rocks, out of which God, hidden in clouds, hands him the tablets of the Law, but in the painting the scene has widened in its symbolism. The dark rock before which Moses, with his enlightened green face, takes the golden tablets into his hands, still defines the composition of the picture, but to the right, under a dark star above which floats a red bird, appear, in a ghostly golden light falling across the right half of the canvas like a reflection of the golden tablets, the Jewish people, standing rapt in this radiance as devout spectators. The scene of Moses receiving the Law, hidden in darkness and the wilderness, becomes the vision of the chosen people, who count themselves the elect because of this scene.

In the shadows of the rock are two singular figures. To the right sits a Jew with the Torah roll. He has every right to be there, because in the Torah the archaic Law is preserved and completed. But at the lower left we find the painter himself, embraced by a figure from his pictures. He too has a place in the golden circle of the divine Law; although it is very obscure and marginal, it is still nearer to the holy one than that of the marveling people in the light. The same is true for the man with the Torah. This metaphorical marginal note shows us how much the painter as a person felt himself involved in his religious picture cycle. Out of the close interaction between life and faith, as the enveloping aura of existence, and art, which grows out of both, has developed the strange personal iconography which distinguishes Chagall's religious pictures and makes him unique in the history of religious art.

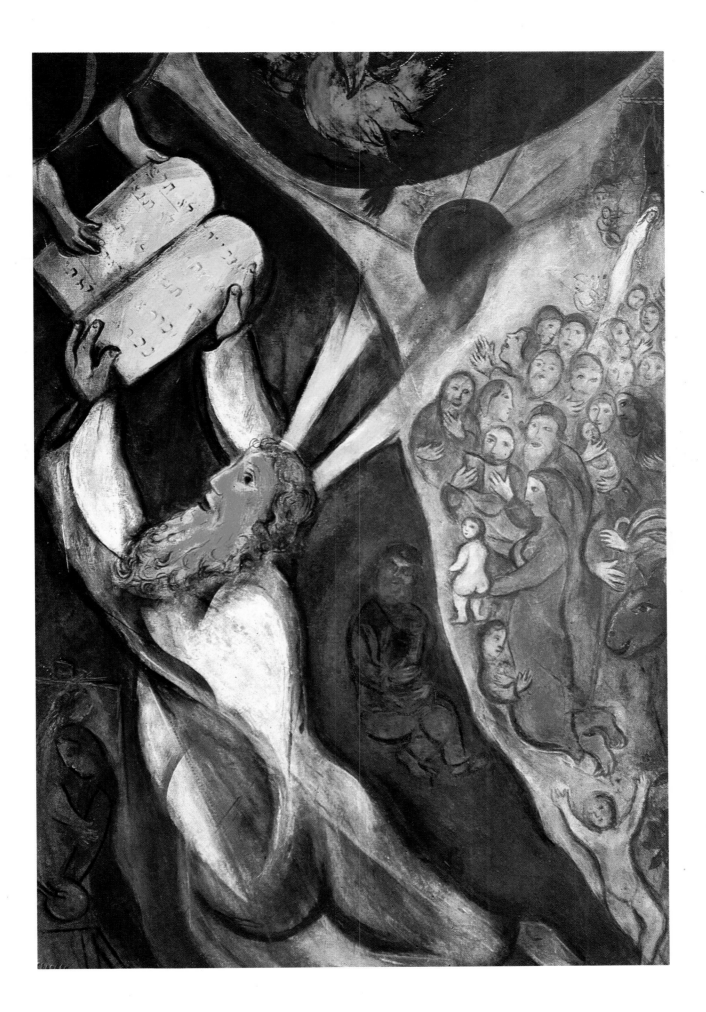

Painted 1962–63

KING DAVID
(Le roi David)

Oil on canvas, 70⅞×38⅝"
Collection the artist

Although it was not until the 1930s that Chagall began to develop his biblical picture cycle, he had been familiar from infancy with the Bible as the history book of the Jews. Like a string of pearls threading his childhood days, the Jewish festivals, full of secret expectations and pleasantly awesome thrills, constantly brought the Bible stories and characters to life again. As in the naive mythology of Christian children such figures as the guardian angel, the Virgin Mary, or even Father Christmas really and truly exist, so for little Marc only a flimsy screen divided his real world from the figures of the Bible: any night the prophet Elijah might have come down in his fiery chariot and landed in the backyard—only it was best not to watch him. This childlike naiveté—that is, the ability to see through reality to the legendary background beyond it—is something Chagall has treasured all his life. There is nothing, it seems to him, to stop those heroes, holy men, and prophets from turning up in real life in a variety of disguises; all one has to do is recognize them, as Abraham did the angels.

In addition, another and much further-reaching idea, of ancient Jewish origin, lives in his heart. This is the idea contained in a wonderful Hasidic parable which tells that, when the flow of God's love poured forth into the basin of the earth, it shattered into the myriad fragments of individual things, in each of which still lives a spark of the divine love. Thus even the most ordinary and commonplace thing preserves a mythical aura, which, if one is a painter, asks to be expressed in the process of transforming visible things by means of the "chemistry" of painting. How much more, then, will not this mythical presence pervade animate life?

Out of such a variety of associations grew the pictures of the Biblical Message which were painted in Vence. They do not adhere very closely to the biblical text and often play quite freely with the biblical figures. The most astonishing example of this is offered by the picture here, *King David*. The figure of David was a perfect subject for Chagall's roving fantasy. Not only was he a brilliant hero, killer of lions, and conqueror of Goliath, but also a great lover who, in his love for Bathsheba—who bore him the king of all kings, Solomon— did not stop short of crime. He was also a great singer and dancer, who eased the heartache of King Saul with his music, sang the poignant lamentation for his friend Jonathan slain by the Philistines, and entered Jerusalem singing and dancing before the Ark of the Covenant.

This King David now appears like a sleepwalking giant, advancing in rhythmic dance steps and playing the harp—a mythical figure in an extraordinary setting in which dream and reality intermingle. Below, in the violet twilight before a side scene of Vence, advances a jubilant, gesticulating procession of godly Jews. To the right, however, floats a bridal pair such as had appeared in Chagallian imagery since 1947 as an emblem of yearning love—strangely elongated in a Mannerist fashion reminiscent of El Greco; also the coloring and buildup recall El Greco or Tintoretto. In the background, before a coulisse of Vitebsk outlined against a stormy sky lit by a golden moon, advances a bridal procession under a red canopy. The two festive processions—one celebrating divine love, the other nuptial love, in which, according to ancient Jewish teaching, the love of God is present—meet in a unity of space and time possible only in the artificial dimension of painting. It seems perfectly natural for such unusual scenes to call forth King David, that he may lead the procession before the Ark of the Covenant, singing and dancing as in days of old. The biblical figure has been resurrected on a legendary level into the circle of the living. In a companion picture of similar dimensions painted in the same year, David kneels before a bridelike Bathsheba, with the Place de la Concorde in Paris as background.

One cannot esteem this artistic event too highly. After centuries of zealous opposition to painting, representation, and portrayals, the Jewish soul has suddenly bared its own legend in the form of painting. This was what Chagall achieved, when, as a painter, he desired to make his religious dream visible. As Jean Leymarie wrote in the preface to the unforgettable exhibition of 1962 at the Musée Rath in Geneva which showed Chagall's entire cycle of biblical pictures, "By making a fresh start on a task which had been left in such a hopeless situation it seemed to have been postponed indefinitely, Chagall reached out beyond the frontiers of his century and accomplished, without betraying either the one or the other, a synthesis never previously achieved of the Jewish culture, which for long had remained indifferent to painting, and modern painting, which had become a stranger to the Bible."

Painted 1966

PORTRAIT OF VAVA
(Portrait de Vava)

Oil on canvas, 36¼×25⅝″
Collection Mme Valentine Chagall, Saint-Paul-de-Vence

Portraits in the conventional documentary or representative sense have never been of interest to Chagall, and the same is true of his landscapes, where anything documentary is very rarely found. He has always refused commissions for portraits. Even his admired teacher Bakst was turned down, when in 1911 in Paris he would have liked Chagall to paint his portrait, in order to help him financially.

Nevertheless, there is a long row of self-portraits, beginning with the self-portrait with a mask of 1908, and countless portraits from his closest circle of family and friends. People had to be very closely connected to him to induce him to portray them. Then, impressive portraits materialized which poetically transfigure the intimate association existing between him and his model and which try to capture the prevailing mood or atmosphere rather than merely rendering a likeness.

In 1909–10, after returning to familiar surroundings upon finishing his studies at art school, where among other things he had copied heads and drawn the models like everyone else, he painted portraits of his sisters, his father, and of course his fiancée Bella, including the celebrated portrait *My Fiancée in Black Gloves* of 1909. Then again in 1914, when he had returned from Paris to Vitebsk and his family and could not leave because of the outbreak of war, he painted, as already mentioned in the text, not only a large group of self-portraits, but countless pictures of members of his family: his mother asleep, outstretched on the divan, or busy at the oven; his grandmother, sisters, brothers, brothers-in-law, and uncles; and the whole Jewish family clan. It was as though he were reclaiming possession of the whole domestic milieu he had missed so much for such a long time, and which could be extended to include the street cleaners, peddlers, and pilgrims who occasionally visited the house when passing through. Above all it was Bella, now his wife, who constantly inspired him to the loveliest and also the boldest figurative compositions of these Russian years, such as the exuberant *Double Portrait with Wineglass* of 1917–18 (fig. 24). In the following years in Paris more portraits of Bella appeared, and soon of their daughter Ida, too (fig. 26). But they became less frequent, and when Bella died in 1944, the theme seemed to have ended, too.

In 1952 Chagall married Valentine Brodsky, affectionately known as Vava, and with that the portraiture began afresh. Between 1953 and 1956 he painted a first portrait, of considerable exactitude, of Vava in the studio, with the picture *Red Roofs* in the background. From then on her oval face appeared more and more often in his fanciful scenes—as angel, muse, or bride. The portrait reproduced here was painted in 1966, among the latest pictures from Vence, as if in gratitude to Vava, who had become the center of his domestic life during those years.

It is a very hallucinated portrait, laying less stress on likeness than on the human significance of her role as guardian and muse. The green face—which to Chagall always means enlightenment and hallucination—is the focus of the picture: it is a beautiful oval face with steadfast eyes, the head resting on the strong pillar of the neck. Alert, attentive, and very composed, Vava sits as a half-figure occupying the foremost plane, as if screening off the painter's dream world, yet with another side of her personality wholly belonging to it. Chagall has therefore placed in her lap the attribute of a diminutive loving couple, his characteristic image for intimate happiness. Behind her this dream world is developed fully. To the left is a scene of Vitebsk by night, with a crescent moon, and a fabulous fish flying across the sky. To the right is Paris with the Opéra, for which Chagall had quite recently painted ceiling panels, together with his beloved emblem for Paris, the Eiffel Tower. Once again, there is a tribute to the two places, Vitebsk and Paris, which had inspired his work. A red animal head and the yellowish face of a girl in profile complete the imagery.

The picture is strongly constructed, and firmly fixed within its borders. Chagall has always made a point of giving the formal and color construction first importance, even in his dreamiest inventions. He has also insisted that his fabulous creatures have no "literary" meaning, nor even an exclusively "metaphorical" one, but rather that they are the building stones of formal and poetic construction. The animal head here is a case in point: without its fiery red the whole color scheme would lose its brilliance. Only through this red does Vava's green face obtain its spiritual light and become the focal point of the constructive and poetic organization.

Painted 1967

LUNARIA
(Les monnaies du Pape)

Oil on canvas, 39⅜ × 31⅞"
Private collection, Paris

Soon after Chagall had moved to Saint-Paul-de-Vence in 1967, he painted two very calm and for him quite unusual pictures. These are two still-life paintings with large flower arrangements which fill the entire picture plane. Without any figures or the extra anecdotal touches with which he had previously delighted to adorn his flower pieces, they evoke nothing but the peaceful existence of the flowers themselves. Behind the flowers is a view of the bright but still empty studio, with a large window opening on to a little grove. As if the painter were listening to this calmness and wanting to take possession personally of his new home, he has left his entire mythical entourage outside and has begun only with the feeling which he has always had—a deep veneration of the beauty of nature.

The still life reproduced here shows a large bunch of lunaria stretching out **across** the entire surface of the picture like sparkling foam. The silvery flicker sets the color tone and modulates the entering light in the finest and lightest gradations. Daintily and fleetingly, by the swift rhythm of the brush, the foliage takes shape and, like a swarm of butterflies, plays against the flaky brightness of the white. The light seems to set the plane into pulsating motion and conveys a sense of movement and transparency without any special perspectival aids. Even the window, which should be the source of this light, is indicated by only the thinnest strokes and seems to cling to the surface. Thus out of the color alone streams the light of the picture. Below, standing solemn and lovely in the center, is a pot of purple cyclamen, its brilliance brought out by a complementary green. The strong accent of these purple flowers shows up the flaky glitter of the white and also forms a delicate association with the four pink, still-covered, discs of lunaria. At the left, magnificently drawn, is a basket of golden-yellow fruit, which leads to the complementary blue of the window zone. The color scheme is quite restrained and is always in keeping with the shining white of the lunaria; there is more a play of feeling than an exercise in color sequence.

Despite this restraint, the picture is a masterpiece of color. One might call it "impressionistic" but miss the point altogether, since every dab of color means not only the thing itself but also the poetic aura lying in and around it. The color transforms reality into its poetic counterpart. In the new studio, which Chagall greeted with a festive bouquet, a bold and free development of color was going to take place.

Painted 1967

THE BLUE FACE
(Le visage bleu)

Oil on canvas, 51⅛ × 38⅛″
Collection A. Maeght, Paris

This very lyrical picture gives a cautious intimation of Chagall's new coloristic enterprise. It is developed from a purely abstract disposition of colors. Without thinking of any particular objective theme, the painter has prepared an attractively colored and harmoniously arranged ground, which serves as the playground for various poetic inventions. With a certain artistic pleasure in the difficulty involved in creating every symmetrical arrangement, he has divided the picture fairly accurately into two vertical halves. At the left he has set up a color zone of dreamy spiritual blue, and by modulating the tone values has given the effect of spatial movement without disturbing the surface. The clearly marked triangular form of deep blue defines the solid frontal plane, behind which is a flat, diffused graduation of planes caused by the distance effect of the light values. At the right, the surface is white and bright, with a variety of faint movements from the freely disposed color planes of earthen yellow, light pink, and bright green, which create a country-like, summery tone.

This well-organized and quite abstractly structured colored ground is, so to speak, the bed of the picture, where many a play of associations may occur. On the left a face takes shape, looking across into the bucolic atmosphere of the multicolored zone, the hand already a part of the bright area. Behind the dark blue triangle is a woman's face and some little Russian huts in a dreamy blue light. In the lower left, however, the painter is at work, standing before his easel and looking across into the bright zone. It is the homely sphere of the painter's own dreams—his familiar surroundings, which he always likes to characterize by the image of his wife's face,

his memories, his work—from which he looks at the world around him. What he sees there—or what he chooses to see at this time—is a tender dream of simple country life. This was a constantly recurring dream, which particularly haunted him in Greece. Above the shyly exploring hand rises a wonderful bouquet of country flowers. To the right stands a peasant woman carrying her child. At the top right, a young country lad plays his flute, and a girl teases a small yellow cow. There is an atmosphere of folklore and fable in these little scenes.

What the unconscious play with color has brought about, therefore, is a tenderly naive metaphor. It is a metaphor on the correspondence between the spiritual life and the simple beauty of the world, made without any literary allusion and appearing "as if of its own accord" only through the color tones and their suggestions.

This purely pictorial metaphor has always been Chagall's special concern, but now it moves somewhat further into the field of color. It was André Breton who said that "with Chagall alone, metaphor made its triumphal entry into modern painting." It would not be out of place to think also of Paul Klee, who during his later period found his way by similar means to similar pictorial parables and metaphors. Chagall was always very fond of Paul Klee, a colleague of his generation, and Klee looked on him in the same way. I find it both enlightening and pleasant, however, as an insight into the painting in our century, that a master like Chagall, whose starting point and development were so completely different from Klee's, quite unexpectedly gives this salute in his direction.

Painted 1968

THE BIG CIRCUS
(Le grand cirque)

Oil on canvas, 66⅞×63″
Pierre Matisse Gallery, New York City

Once Chagall had settled down to work in the new studio in Saint-Paul, the old circus theme cropped up again.

Ever since his childhood, when he had seen the acrobats in the streets of the little Russian provincial town, this theme never let him go. It signified the sudden invasion of the wondrous into the rhythm of everyday life, or the transformation of the humdrum into artistry, without any particular aim yet leaving behind a lingering sensation of happiness and amazement. For Chagall, all this seemed to have an allegorical connection with his own art and its performance, and also with his own complicated-naive character, for he could never feel himself to be a painter alone, but also an *artiste*, magician, actor, and clown.

Sometimes the circus theme turned up more often because of outside influences. For instance in 1927, midway through the illustrations to the *Fables* of La Fontaine, Vollard suddenly invited him to illustrate the circus theme; night after night, Chagall sat with the famous old editor enjoying the Cirque d'Hiver. And in 1956 in Vence, he was invited to attend the shooting of a circus film in the Cirque d'Hiver; this aroused fresh interest in the theme, and the major result was the famous *Big Circus* of 1956, a prodigious canvas measuring 59 by 122 inches. But apart from such highlights, the theme runs throughout his work.

In 1967 Chagall painted an enchanting little picture, *The Circus Ring (La piste de cirque)*, wholly composed of red, yellow, and green, looking in its compact, enameled style of painting like a tribute to Georges Rouault. The picture illustrated here followed in 1968, and is the largest easel painting of that year.

It is the most extraordinary of all the circus pictures. The basic color tone is determined by black and white. The effect is impressively dramatic and deeply serious. The rhythmic pattern of the arcs and the surrounding composition has a strangely solemn—one might almost say Byzantine—quality, such as we find in Chagall's sacred windows. Bordering the black-and-white zone on either side are abstractly located color planes of cool green, and on the upper right-hand side the strip of terrestrial green is set off by a panel of nocturnal blue. Like curtains, these color zones screen off the spiritual realm of the vision. But the suggestions of these varied colors, occurring in abstractly placed panels without regard to objective coloring, in the coloristic method used by Chagall at this period, have the effect of transforming the black and white into color—into glistening light and darkness. In terms of color, the drama is already staged.

Below is revealed the half-circle of the arena, in which a girl stunt rider, standing on the back of a horse with a cock's head, plays the violin. Behind them is the ring of onlookers and musicians, and to the right is a clown playing the clarinet. All that is fairly normal. The really remarkable event takes place up above, where an angel with gigantic wings comes swooping down from the heavenly zone. Its mitral headdress and the Jewish ritual instruments identify this being as a messenger of God. Protectively and yet fatefully it bows over the circus scene. A heavenly horse seeks to fraternize with his circus companion with the cock's head. Meanwhile, at the upper right, in the field of spiritual blue, the female figure who a moment ago seemed to be a circus rider now appears transformed into a bridelike angel floating upward. To the right at the top, there is a most remarkable emblem: a hand in the segment of a sphere, sending a ray of blessing across to the angel of destiny. According to Byzantine iconography, it is the hand of God. But doesn't it hold a brush? And don't the motley dabs at the edge of the circle suggest a painter's palette? Definitely not—apart from the religious idea that in the vision of the artist there will always be a glimmer of divine enlightenment, as was always claimed by the pious Jewish Hasidim. In this way, the picture becomes a far-reaching metaphor, with the circus becoming the world theater. And the painter himself? He becomes God's clown.

Painted 1968

EASTER
(Pâques)

Oil on canvas, 63×63"
Collection the artist

Religion is never out of Chagall's mind. He carries his faith around with him wherever he goes, just as the wandering Jew—that recurrent figure of his personal mythology—carries his sack. The biblical message and the festive circle of the Jewish year inexorably demanded of him that he should constantly bear witness; this theme runs throughout his art.

In *Easter* of 1968, painted in the studio at Saint-Paul, the theme appears in the highly dramatic coloring with which the painter was wholly occupied at this period. Here again black and white set the basic tone, which is heightened to a visionary light by the mysteriously shining red plane. Like a window, it opens on a blood-red star, with a cold complementary green enhancing its fiery glow still further.

Whenever the Jewish religious festivals occupied Chagall's imagination, the memory of his homeland seemed to return of its own accord, so closely were the expectations of his childhood governed by the Jewish festive rites. So here too we find the Russian village, the suburb of Vitebsk. There are the wooden houses, huddled together, a little lamp glowing faintly in one of their windows; a woman steps outside the door, a winged creature peeps over the rooftop, a solitary couple wanders up the village street in the dusk. An enormous white moon pours its cold light like snowflakes over the houses. To the left, four old Jews keep the feast of the Passover, huddled in their prayer shawls beneath this icy light. They sit in the open field, above which a stormy sky drives the thin crescent moon. How exposed and threatened is their existence and their festive ritual in this coldness! But once again an angel rises up and with its wings covers the menace of the blood-red star. Peering out of the dark lattice, its yellow color transfiguring the ghostly light and also affecting the angel, an animal's head observes the phenomenon in the heavenly zone with astonishment.

There is a great deal of menace in this picture, much compassion for suffering, and only a little consolation. The drama of threatened human existence, saved only by its faith, is completely bared. It is heightened to a universal allegory by the constructive power of color, and it may well be that the glowing colors of Chagall's sacred windows—the effect of the black strips of lead against the translucent stained glass—put Chagall on this road to dramatic color effects in painting.

Painted 1968

THE MAGICIAN
(Le magicien)

Oil on canvas, 55⅛×58¼"
Private collection

The year 1968 was one of great coloristic effort for Chagall. His determination to give full rein to the play of color is remarkable; he now set about the task of breaking open the tightly woven color web of his pictures and then of greatly intensifying the effect of the basic harmonies developed from adjacent colors by the disturbance and counterbalance of freely interposed, firmly outlined, and sharply colored areas.

The memory of the methods of Orphic Cubism practiced in his early period, in which an independent, aperspective pictorial dimension was built up from initially abstract color planes in low-relief layers, may have proved helpful and encouraged him to try new experiments. Another factor may have been Juan Gris's idea of developing the picture as an abstract arrangement of colors and shapes, and "objectively qualifying" the emerging color forms only as the work progressed. In this way, the "discovered" object is given the poetic dimension of an "appearance" through pictorial means alone.

Chagall was well acquainted with the procedure of developing his picture fables out of the suggestions of color. What concerned him now was heightening the tension of the color by the insertion of dramatic dissonances, in such a way that the meaning—the Chagallian mythology—was also enhanced. Thus he painted a small group of very bold and comparatively experimental pictures, including *The Green Farm (La ferme en vert)* and *The Rainbow Cock (Le coq arc-en-ciel)*; of this group *The Magician* is the major work.

On an almost monochrome ground, prismatically fragmented and faceted like a crystal, the picture shows a panoramic view of Paris, with the Seine bridges, the Place de la Concorde and the Madeleine, Sacré Coeur, and the Eiffel Tower; at the upper left is the Opéra, which Chagall has particularly liked to include in his pictures since he painted the panels for its enormous ceiling in 1964. In the middle, embedded in nocturnal blue, lies a loving couple. But this peaceful world is disrupted by an unusual performance, glittering in many colors, which provokes the appearance of a new and unexpected figure. On the blue ground Chagall has painted sharply outlined bright-colored areas, which look as if they had been cut out with scissors, comparable to *papiers découpés*. Out of these "color cut-outs" he has constructed on the right an odd figure, quite alien to the familiar Chagallian iconography. Palette-like shapes associated with the figure seem to indicate the painter, but various other strange instruments, together with the bearded, gleaming-white prophet's head, suggest a different meaning. Here the magician takes the stage—as the principal figure, stepping out in front of the ensemble. There is a deep-red quadrangle on the left to ensure a balanced arrangement of color, and two bright bunches of flowers to counterbalance the diagonal color trend.

Through this artistic manipulation an entirely new plane has been created, a kind of proscenium in front of the blue ground, a domain of meaning where the magician alone holds sway. Through this artistic device, the picture world of the blue ground is given a greater and more mysterious depth; it is transported into the visionary sphere and is manifested in the magic prism of the faceted surface. The magician-artist, who is the painter, transforms the visible world into pure poetry. This is the metaphorical meaning which finally emerges from the play with heightened color.

Chagall has taken some drastic measures in this picture, and its experimental character cannot be denied. Yet here the artistic and suggestive possibilities of color and its innate dramatic power have been pushed so far that, even if the dramatic subject matter were taken away, a new eloquence of color would remain. The result of a more restrained concept is shown in *The Sun of Poros* (colorplate 39), the largest painting in this group.

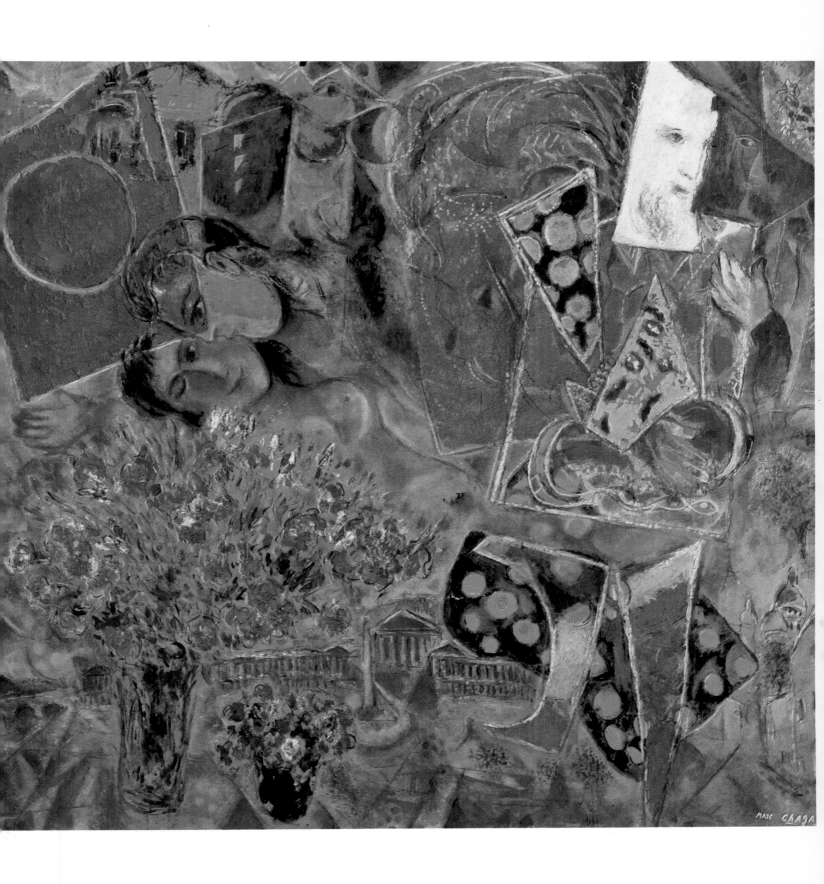

Painted 1968

THE SUN OF POROS
(Le soleil de Poros)

Oil on canvas, 63×63″
Collection the artist

This picture was painted in 1968, but its title recalls happy days of long ago spent on the Greek island of Poros. In 1968 Chagall was engaged in the completion of the vast Odysseus mosaic (fig. 58) for the new Faculty of Law building in Nice, and being thus occupied with the Greek theme and occasionally looking through the gouaches he had made in Greece, he may have remembered his trips to Greece—as if looking through a window. Indeed, within the almost abstract arrangement of color fields, on the right-hand side of the picture within the expanse of purple, Chagall has drawn an open window, in which appears the vague shape of an island under the hot sun of Apollo.

Chagall had visited Poros in 1952 and again in the autumn of 1954. The publisher Tériade, Vollard's heir and thus the inheritor of the series of etchings Chagall had made for Vollard, had urged the painter to illustrate the antique pastoral romance *Daphnis and Chloe* with color lithographs. Tériade wanted the Greek island as a background to these illustrations, and invited Chagall to come and live in his house on Poros. For a while the painter was undecided, for at that time the world of Greece was unknown to him, but, just as he had felt it necessary to go to Palestine before starting on the biblical etchings, he had also felt it was essential for him to become acquainted with the location of his new and very intriguing task.

His first journey to the island took him through Athens and Delphi. The impression was overwhelming. The light of Greece breathing over the simple structure of the landscape, with both forming a perfect background to the graceful severity of the archaic sculpture, captivated him completely. And he now realized that this world of Greece was the other pillar supporting Western culture, which until then the temple of Jerusalem had obscured from his view. He never forgot this. At that time he made the first gouaches and pastels—simple landscapes—but these were followed by the gouaches of the journey of 1954 which later served as designs for the litho-

graphs to *Daphnis and Chloe*. He used the antique theme once more in 1958 when he designed the scenery for Ravel's ballet *Daphnis and Chloe* for the Paris Opéra. Then it receded for almost ten years. But the poetry of the world of Greece and the memory of that wonderful "breathing" light lingered in his heart and mind, resurfacing now and then, particularly in landscapes made in Vence; *The Sun of Poros* bears witness to this process.

As an artistic undertaking it is almost unique among Chagall's later works, and in the formal problems it poses it may be compared with *The Magician* (colorplate 38), made in the same year. Rigorously laid out in an almost geometric arrangement of colored surface fields, it seeks to establish at the outset a self-sufficient balance of color values, covering the whole range of the color circle: from green to red, from yellow to blue, with the greatest weight being given to the sonorous black on the left-hand side. The distance values of the pure colors breathe life into the surface and define it objectively: there, as the blue of the sky; here, in the vibrant purple of the sunrise, as a glimpse of some remembered Greek scene. It is the suggestive power of color which brings about the poetic-objective definition: a window opens onto the purple landscape, in front of which, in celebration of this appearance, is set a bouquet of country flowers from Vence, rising up out of the green field. Below, in the brown field, sleeps a dreaming girl, and above her, as if seen in her dream, a loving couple rises out of the black field into the radiant blue of the night, as a now universal allegory for which Daphnis and Chloe had stood in earlier times. Out of the black field, a spectral white cow bellows at the rising sun. In a kind of automatic chain one metaphor summons up the next, and at the end of this associative exploration of the color dimension, evoked solely by the significance of the purple apparition, the meaning emerges—the title marks not the beginning but the end of the work: *The Sun of Poros*.

Made 1967–68

THE MESSAGE OF ODYSSEUS (detail)
(Le message d'Ulysse)

Wall mosaic, 9'10"×36'
Faculté de Droit et des Sciences Economiques de l'Université, Nice

In January 1967, the Dean of the Faculty of Law at the University of Nice requested Chagall to make a wall picture for the Faculty's newly erected building; Chagall agreed to the idea, and they settled on a mosaic. Chagall had recently worked on a large mosaic for the new Parliament of Israel, and was thus familiar with the technique. In Nice, a wide corridor on the first floor, leading to the lecture rooms, offered a suitable wall measuring 9'10"×36' which, with its windows opening on the coast and the sea, presented a desirable connection with the Mediterranean scene.

Chagall had just made a present of his Biblical Message—a series of large pictures on Old Testament themes—to the city of Nice, and now wished to present the young students not only with a work of art but with a comparable message. The Dean of the Faculty suggested the theme of "Odysseus, Mediterranean hero of wisdom," referring to the essays by Gabriel Andisio, published in 1945, *Ulysse ou l'intelligence*. He also suggested a group of suitable scenes—Calypso, Polyphemus, Circe, the Sirens, Nausicaa, the return to Ithaca—which exemplify overcoming all temptations and cruelties by virtue, courage, and wisdom, and the final triumph of humanity, freedom, and peace.

This proposal met with Chagall's full approval. During his visits to Greece in 1952 and 1954, he had marveled at the strength and sweetness of the Greek landscape and its mythical background, and had come to realize that the Acropolis in Athens was the necessary counterpart to the temple in Jerusalem; the brightness and lively vigor of everything Greek formed the counterpoint to the solemn holy splendor of Jerusalem. All the richness of Western culture stems from their interaction. With the Odysseus theme Chagall wanted to depict "the multiple sources of the Mediterranean soul," according to the inscription carved in the marble dedication plaque. But the message for mankind was to be that man, through wisdom, courage, and faith, can overcome all his trials and, like Odysseus in Ithaca, be able in freedom and peace to fulfill his human responsibility—the care of his home and the service of the community.

By the end of May 1967—the work having been interrupted only by a brief visit to New York for the opening of *The Magic Flute*, for which Chagall had designed the scenery—the finished design, measuring 29⅞×96⅛", was ready. The execution was put into the hands of the Parisian mosaicist Lino Melano, who had previously worked on the mosaic for the Parliament of Israel. The materials having been procured—some of them very costly, such as onyx, cupreous minerals, and gilded glass from Murano—work on the mosaic started at the beginning of March 1968, under the supervision of Chagall. Five months later, on August 6, it was finished (fig. 58).

Chagall included all the scenes mentioned to him. He even extended them by adding the assembly of the gods on Olympus at which Athena asks Zeus to aid her protégé, in order to emphasize by this scene the dispensation of divine providence in the fate of man. To bring this assemblage of scenes into a legendary context, Chagall placed the giant central figure of the sleeping Odysseus, filling the whole height of the picture, in the middle of the scene, as a dreaming, garlanded hero, seeing the stations of his life passing before him. Left and right, as on the sides of an iconostasis, the individual scenes unfold, but overflow into one another without interruption. They begin with the convention of the gods at the upper left and continue in the upper row with the scenes of Calypso, the blinding of Polyphemus, Circe, and the Sirens. The sequence continues in the lower row, beginning from the left, with Nausicaa, the killing of the suitors, the marriage chamber (as the nucleus of intimate happiness), and the peaceful death of Odysseus in the circle of his kinfolk. Above them, characteristic of Chagall's wide-ranging iconography, appears a seraph with outstretched arms in the form of a cross.

The cast of characters has been reduced to a few principal figures, and only a few signs for pillars and temples indicate the classical background. The drawing of the figures follows a familiar Chagallian picture pattern: Calypso, lying in her blue-gold grotto by the sea, appears as the "lover," or Odysseus in the same scene as the "grieving thinker"; these are figures taken from the inventory of his imagination which, in the course of his life's work, have become signs or formulas for particular human emotions, and which occur repeatedly in both the profane and the biblical pictures. The superficial staging of this mosaic with its numerous figures has something in common with the monumental wall pictures which Chagall had produced in recent years: in 1959 the *Commedia dell'arte* for the theater in Frankfurt, in 1964 the ceiling panels for the Paris Opéra (figs. 54–57), in 1965 the murals for the Metropolitan Opera in New York.

But entirely different, corresponding to the Greek atmosphere of the Homeric poem, is the color and spatial buildup of the surface, which seems to move in waves. Out of the movement of color alone it designs a cosmic landscape filled with the sound of the sea, whose light blue recurs throughout the design. Over the clear-colored ground the color blends here and there into green, thus evoking the idea of islands and shores; mixes with gold and brings a picture of mysterious sea grottoes to mind; or intones a bloody red where the pictorial drama requires it, as in the scene with Polyphemus. Out of the color a kind of counterpart landscape comes into being, which renders the view of sea and shore outside the windows poetically and mythically. By this means the mythical scenes have room to unfold. The individual mythological scenes are completely embedded in the color movements; they emerge like figurative incarnations of the mood and motion of the color.

The detail here, showing the head of the dreaming Odysseus, can give only a rough impression of the brilliance and richness of the color sequence. It does show, however, how the concise abbreviated drawing blends entirely with the close, tapestry-like web of the color and is actually raised up by the movements of the color. "*Il faut fondre,*" cried Chagall to his mosaic workers, "*il faut faire chanter le dessin par la couleur, il faut faire comme Debussy, comme Debussy.*" That is the watchword of a great colorist, who becomes a narrator only by way of the color, and only by means of color turns the anecdote into a picture.

Photographic Credits

Archives Photographiques (Paris): fig. 8; Jean Arlaud: fig. 11;
P. Bijtebier (Brussels): fig. 29; Colin (Vence): figs. 2, 6, 42–52;
Colten (New York City): fig. 33; J. Dubout (Paris): figs. 54–57;
R. Gautier: fig. 31; Luc Joubert (Paris): fig. 40; H. Kahn (Los
Angeles): fig. 28; Kleinhempel (Hamburg): fig. 9; Panda: fig. 4;
J.D. Schiff (New York City): fig. 14; J.R. Simkin (Antibes): fig. 58;
M. Vaux (Paris): fig. 17.